A VISION FOR HUMANITY

MOVING MANKIND IN THE RIGHT DIRECTION

A Book of Hope and Inspiration

JASON SHOHARA

With Guest Introduction by
Lauren E. Shiro

"Your story is our priority"

LitPrime Solutions
21250 Hawthorne Blvd
Suite 500, Torrance, CA 90503
www.litprime.com
Phone: 1-800-981-9893

Published by LitPrime Solutions   03/30/2023

ISBN: 979-8-88703-213-9(sc)
ISBN: 979-8-88703-214-6(hc)
ISBN: 979-8-88703-215-3(e)

Library of Congress Control Number: 2023906110

Dedicated To
The People of the World

*If you can only see and accept
what I see in a person with love.*
Jason Shohara

CONTENTS

ACKNOWLEDGEMENTS

I am grateful to many people in my life who have inspired and supported me to write this book. First and foremost is my gratitude to my wife *Marie* who didn't kick me out of the bedroom when I frequently went to bed in the wee hours in the morning writing this book.

I also want to thank my former pastor at First Friends Church of Whittier, California, *Becky Memmelaar* and her husband *Ron,* both whom have been very supportive of my efforts but particularly of Becky who has given me a tremendous amount of spiritual insight during Meeting for Worship on Sunday mornings. Also, to my spiritually uplifting friends both in the choir and in the congregation at First Friends Church, a Quaker Meeting

A special thanks to *Author Grant Schnarr* and my extended friends and followers of Emanuel Swedenborg. My special gratitude for introducing me to Mr. Swedenborg's writings through his works at the 2010 *Los Angeles Times* Festival of Books and bringing to my attention the connection of him (Swedenborg) and my favorite place to meditate, the Wayfarers Chapel in Pacific Palisades, California.

I also cannot ignore the person who originally gave me

the inspiration to write this book from our conversational interview on Facebook in 2010, *Mr. Leandus Poe* of the Million Dollar Book Reviews and my many friends there whom not only honored me with their prestigious People's Choice Award, but also gave me the inspiration to continue to "move man in the right direction."

Also to my dear friend and author *Deshon Fox*, whose book *The Middle Theory – A Guide to Balance,* has taught me a tremendous importance and need for balance in this world in all aspects of life.

It would be a mistake to ignore my dearest friend and author *Lauren Shiro* who has continually encouraged me to push ahead with this book – often when I had encountered episodes of writer's block. And who has graciously accepted the task to write the guest introduction to this book. Hugs to my dear friend, Lauren!

To a special friend and classmate from Montebello High School, *Linda Capps Atchison* (Reno, NV) who had generously donated towards the vision of humanity and the cause of moving mankind in the right direction. I only hope that this effort will be fruitful and successful.

To my editor, *Rob Bignell*, who once again had provided his wonderful services by editing this book as he did for my first novel, *Kami Jin*. I thank you once again from the bottom of my heart.

To everyone whom I've met in the world who has taught me that we are all connected.

I also express my deepest gratitude and appreciation to you, *dear reader*. May you find the courage and willingness to inspire others to awake and become aware of their surroundings and join our effort and dialogue to move mankind in the right direction. Join the dialogue to create mankind's greatest dream and destiny. For after reading this book, hopefully you will find the power to make changes with your fellow men in the spirit of creating humanity's greatest vision – a better new world. Spread the word! Get active in your communities, on the Internet, social media channels like Facebook, Twitter, YouTube, LinkedIn, Google+, blogs, etc. We can change the world for the better. And for the world's sake, we need to wake people up from their slumbers and lead them into ascension!

GUEST INTRODUCTION

When I was initially asked to write the introduction to this book, I was both flattered and unsure of myself. What does someone say regarding a work such as this?

In my opinion, a book like this should not need to be written. It should be simply understood that we are all equal; that there is only one race: the human race. Sadly, though, the reality is, this book is necessary. Somehow, we have lost sight of the unity of mankind. Who better to remind us of who we really are than Jason Shohara?

He is a man who passes no judgment. He looks at every person he meets and all he sees is the person, not a color, gender, or orientation. He refuses to label anyone. In that regard, he is a true inspiration to us all. He shows us what it really means to be human. Instead of picking apart our few differences, he highlights our infinite similarities.

I love that in this book, Mr. Shohara reminds us that all belief systems share the same principles. I appreciate how he speaks to the unity of all people, regardless of their race, gender or orientation. I revel in his honesty and the beauty behind his words of wisdom and love.

The reality is: he is exactly right. The color of our skin, the belief system we follow, the languages we speak, the music we play are all tiny differences compared to the similarities we as humans share. The DNA in our blood is 99% similar from one person to another. It is only that one per cent that actually separates us. Yes, that one per cent makes us unique. However, it also reminds us that we are really all kin.

As an out member of the LGBT community, and as a minority I have so often wondered why man acted in such hatred and fear of his own kind. Since childhood, I have never been able to comprehend prejudice of any sort. I have always seen people, not races or religions or any other differentials. I knew that as someone who is very much a minority in American society, I hated the ignorance that I was forced to face. I knew that I never wanted to impose that awful feeling on anyone else. As a writer, I have used my craft to create novels and stories that showed us how unfounded ignorance really is. Yet, I find that the voice I have been searching for can be found here, in these words.

This book talks about humanity – human kind and the human connection. In a world of digital photos, virtual conferences and automated voice systems, we have lost that human connection. Ergo, we have lost humanity. In this book, Mr. Shohara brings back the human connection and brings us back to humanity; back to the unity that we as a species so desperately need.

Come join us in a world of open minds and hearts. A world where labels need not apply to anyone. A world where we are all equal. Come join us in this incredible *Vision for Humanity*.

Lauren Shiro, Author and Model
Author: Loving Her; Unbreakable Hostage; Imperfect; Impeccable; Trajectory; Amnesie

PREFACE

After completing my novel, *Kami Jin*, I felt as if I was being urged to write more about my insights that I received from God and shared through the protagonist, Gordon Sakata, while he was surviving in the cold Sierra Nevada Mountains during the segment referred to as the "sermons on the mount." Honestly, that was only the beginning. The spiritual awakening continued throughout the progression of the book when I revealed my vision for a utopian world in contrast to the dystopian Earth which was plagued with poverty and homelessness in the 23rd Century.

Yet, when I finished the book, I felt that the work was still unfinished – there was still a lot of work to be done. Exactly what wasn't too clear until recently when God sent me a message through another author who was interviewing me on Facebook. Up unto the time of the interview, I was frequently struggling to determine exactly what I was supposed to do. In fact, during my 25th wedding anniversary in June, my wife and I celebrated at Disneyland. During my visit there, I was envious of the park employees and often wished that I could have worked in the park in operations after having served in the Entertainment Division for three seasons as a Toy Soldier during *Fantasy on Parade*. An inner voice, however, reminded me that there was a more important task for me to carry out.

Like what? Working in the park would be serving the people well, I thought. But later I found out, the task that was to come before me was even more important. The interview I had on Facebook was a little different than the other author interviews I had during my virtual book tour the previous month. The guest blogging and spotlights were mainly focused on my science fiction novel. The Facebook interview, in particular, focused on me as I shared my experiences with race relations, growing up in a world of hate and discrimination, social and political change, etc. I used part of Dr. Martin Luther King Jr.'s great "I have a dream" speech that he delivered on the steps of the Lincoln Memorial on August 28, 1963 in Washington, D.C. When he delivered the speech, I was young and immature. His words didn't really mean anything at the time. But as I grew older, his speech came alive! And, I admit that I try to make his dream a reality in my daily life.

When I came back home from worship service the Sunday after our anniversary, I opened my email and received an unusual request. I feel that God was using this person as a messenger to relay the mission that He wanted me to do. The message read: "Please continue to move mankind in the right direction."

In the words of the great Bill Cosby, in his famous skit *Noah's Ark:* "Right!"

And so begins this perilous journey. How does one even begin to move mankind? Where does one start? I am not a prophet nor claim to be a figure described in biblical accountings and prophecy. I am only a contemporary servant of God.

So to begin with, let us lay down some ground rules before we get started. First of all, the contents of this book demand an open mind, free from any prejudice of religion, doctrine, or spiritual experience, personal and/or corporate. I encourage you to continue to learn and explore new and exciting experiences. But be vigilant of everything that is happening around you, in your life both socially and politically. Keep your faith regardless of what religious orientation that may be. But be open to clear understanding and utmost tolerance of other views and beliefs. What you have learned in the past *is not the only way*, but just another way. Accept the ultimate goal that we must all come together in oneness by identifying our common beliefs, yet cherish our differences and accomplishments.

Henceforth, each of you must shed your ego for if mankind is to move in the right direction, there is no room for egotism. Our contributions must be made towards the edification of mankind, not just of one country, but the entire world. Therefore, shed your shallow and negative perceptions about people in other countries, across your borders; then, tear down the walls that separate and prevent you from becoming one.

It is very important that this effort be a collaborative effort, not only because there is power in numbers, but the multitudes will be needed to defend against those forces which will try to derail the effort of becoming one. There are talks and rumors that secret organizations and societies are planning to control the world by establishing a One World Government or corporation. Part of their plan is to enslave citizens, levy overburdening taxes, and carry out genocide by population reduction to the degree that this world has never seen in its history. These people do not value human life, but rather profits for a very small percentage of the world's population. These people will carry out their plans at all cost.[i] Citizens of the world must be vigilant and concerned for these people hold the nuclear codes and could very well carryout self-destruction of this

Earth. Watch out for deceptive practices and questionable "natural" disasters which may be "fronts" for something else that may be taking place in the background. Like a grand magic show, these are all illusions causing our eyes to be diverted from one thing, while something else has happened without our knowledge. Carefully monitor the behavior of your elected leaders in government, especially when they promise the people one thing, then renege on their promises or "defer" their commitment to another time. This is not procrastination -- these are stall tactics designed to deceive the observer. Therefore, be continuously watchful and see who is actually pulling the strings in your government.

Of course, many may consider these rumors to be nothing but conspiracy theories and rhetoric. Some will claim it is false prophecy. Yet, others will claim that it is all predicted in Biblical prophecy and by Nostradamus as signs of the "End Times." I am not here to announce the arrival of a doomsday prophecy or anything of the like. The only thing I predicted in my science fiction novel, *Kami Jin*, the end of the world will be man's causing – not God's. And witnessing current events and the behavior of man, I'm led to be even more vigilant on current times and affairs. I highly recommend that you do likewise.

During the course of this book, I'll offer my observations on a few important movements of interest. My hope for this book is to establish bridges and join people towards a common goal of creating oneness and a better world. But, this cannot be accomplished by splintered efforts. That is, there are groups of people with one vision, and other groups with yet another. Yet, these groups are not talking to each other, nor sharing ideas. And, more seriously, ego and attitude is creating a barrier for constructive dialogue, thus tearing each other's ideas apart.

Finally, I'll share my vision for the world as it was given to me by God in preparation for even greater things to come. As a disclaimer, I am not here, nor is the intent of this book to endorse a particular spiritual movement like New Age, or religious domination be it Christianity, Islam, Buddhism, Hinduism, Judaism, or whatever. My intent is not to change your religious beliefs nor force you to accept my concepts and theories. My objective is to get people to shed their differences and find common ground through mutual understanding so that mankind, as a whole, can move in one direction towards oneness – unconditional peace, love, equality, and tranquility.

So, before you begin to read this book, clear your minds of clutter and let go of the things that you have been holding onto from the past. Then, trash the proverbial "label gun." Henceforth, all things will cease to have labels – this includes people of color, race, nationality, creed, religion, sexual orientation, etc. From now on, each individual will be considered as a unique, divine human being with equal inalienable rights guaranteed by the Creator. And, if you don't believe in the Creator, that's fine also! Just keep an open mind for opportunities and possibilities of becoming one – *a human race.*

Jason Shohara
Whittier, California

Namaste.
Or, In the Muslim world, the greeting would commonly be expressed:
"Assalaam Alaikum…"
"Peace be with you…"

SECTION ONE

IN THE BEGINNING

CHAPTER 1

OVERVIEW OF WORLD RELIGIONS

THE MANIFESTATION OF TRUTH THROUGH TIME, CULTURES, AND GENERATIONS

"In the beginning was the Word, and the Word was with God, and the Word was God. He was in the beginning with God."

John 1:1

And thus opens the Gospel According to John. But for centuries, the beginning has often been debated. Exactly when was the beginning? Of course, to Christians, this matter is not debatable. The beginning was when God created the world according to Genesis 1:1. But to non-Christians, the "beginning" may very well be defined as the beginning of their respective religion. Just out of curiosity, let us explore the timeline of the world's religions up through modern day:

History and Timeline of Its Founders[ii]

- 50,000 BCE. Primordial Sumerian Religion of the C'Thulu
- 25,000 BCE. The Sha'Ang Religion of the Pekinese
- 5000 BC. Hindi Vedic Spirituality, Babylonian Mystika
- 2400 BC. Greco-Phonecian Eleusian & Dionysiac Mysticism
- 2,085 BC. Judaism-Abraham
- 2,000 BC. Hinduism- no specific founder
- 560 BC. Buddhism- Gautama Buddha
- 550 BC. Taoism - Lao Tzu
- 599 BC. Jainism, Mahavira
- 30 AD. Christianity –Jesus Christ
- 50-100 AD. Gnosticism-
- 150-250 AD. -Modalism (Monarchianism)– Sabellius, Praxeus, Noetus, Paul of Samosata
- 325 AD. - After being persecuted for almost 200 years Constantine made the Church becomes a legal religion, compromise begins to enter.
- 590 AD. - Roman Catholicism- Developed after Constantine; Pope Gregory?
- 610 AD. – Islam - Mohammed
- 1400 AD. – Rosicrucians - Christian Rosenkreuz (1694 US) Rosicrucians - Master Kelpius, Johann Andrea
- 1515 AD. - Protestantism- (Reformers) Martin Luther, Ulrich Zwingli, John Calvin
- 1650 AD. - Tibetan Buddhism-Dalai Lama
- 1650 AD. – Quakers (Religious Society of Friends) – George Fox
- 1700 AD. – Freemasony - Albert Mackey, Albert Pike

- 1760 AD. - Swedenborgism - Emmanuel Swedenborg
- 1784 AD. - Shakers - Mother Ann Lee
- 1830 AD. - Mormonism – Joseph Smith
- 1830 AD. – Cambellites - Alexander & Thomas Cambell, Barton Stone
- 1838 AD. – Tenrikyo - Miki Maegawa Nakayama
- 1844 AD. – Christadelphians - John Thomas
- 1840 - 45 AD. - Millerites 2nd day Adventists – William Miller then became 7th Day Adventists
- 1844 AD. – Bahai - Baha'u'llah (AbulBaha)
- 1845 - 1870AD. - 7th Day Adventists - E.G. White
- 1848 AD.-Spiritualism - Kate and Margaret Fox
- 1870 AD. - Jehovah's Witnesses - Charles Taze Russell
- 1875 AD. - Theosophical Society - H.P. Blavatsky, Henry Olcott
- 1879 AD. - Christian Science - Mary Baker Eddy
- 1889 - 1924 AD. - Unity School of Christianity - Myrtle Fillmore
- 1900 AD. - Rosicrucian Fellowship - Max Heindel
- 1902 AD. - Anthroposophical Society – Rudolf Steiner
- 1906 AD. - The Pentecostal Assemblies of the World
- 1914 AD. - Iglesiani Cristo - Felix Manalo
- 1914 AD. - Oneness Pentecostalism - Frank Ewart, G.T.Haywood, Glenn Cook

- 1917 AD. - True Jesus Church. Founders Paul Wei, Lingsheng Chang and Barnabas Chang
- 1930 AD. - Black Muslims (Nation of Islam) – Wallace D. Fard
- 1927 AD. - Mind Science - Ernest Holmes
- 1934 AD. - World Wide Church of God - Herbert W. Armstrong
- 1935 AD. - Self Realization Fellowship - Paramahansa Yogananda
- 1954 AD.- Unification Church- Sun Myung Moon
- 1945 AD. - The Way - Victor P.Wierwille
- 1948 AD. - Latter Rain – Franklin Hall, George Warnock.
- 1964 AD. - Eckankar The Ancient Science of Soul Travel (Eck). Founded by Paul Twitchell
- 1968 AD. - Hare Krishna (US) - Swami Prabhupada
- 1968 AD. - Children of God - David (Moses) Berg
- 1945 AD. - United Pentecostal International - Howard Goss, W.T. Witherspoon (can be traced back to 1914)
- 1944 AD. - Silva Mind Control – Jose Silva
- 1950 AD. - Urantia Book - Dr. Bill Sadler
- 1950 AD. - Lafayette Ronald Hubbard published his book Dianetics - SCIENTOLOGY
- 1954 AD. - Atherius Society (UFO's) - Dr. George King
- 1955 AD. – Scientology - L. Ron Hubbard
- 1958 AD. - Institute of Divine Metaphysical Research - Henry Kinley

- 1958 - 1970 AD. - Church Universal and Triumphant – Mark and E.C. Prophet
- 1958 AD. - Henry Kinley begins (IDMR) the Institute of Divine Metaphysical Research
- 1959 AD. - Unitariarian Universalist
- 1960 AD. - Transcendental meditation - Maharishi Mahesh Yogi
- 1961 AD. - Unitarian Universalism was officially formed.
- 1965 AD. - Assembly of Yahweh - Jacob Meyer
- 1970 AD. - Findhorn Community – Peter and Eileen Caddy – David Spangler
- 1970 AD. - Divine light Mission - Guru MaharajJi
- 1973 AD. - CARP was established in the United States. [The Collegiate Association for the Research of Principles] to introduce the teachings of Sun Myung Moon.
- 1974 AD. - Assemblies of Yahweh - Sam Suratt
- 1979 AD. - Church of Christ International - Kip McKean
- 1980 - 1982 AD. - Tara Center - Benjamen Crème
- 1980 AD. - House of Yahweh (Abilene) Jacob Hawkins

So we can see that religions of the world each had their own beginnings, some much older than others. Similarities -- you bet!

Let's start with the negative side of the coin. The commonalities among all religions are that they have differences and disagreements. Some so serious that they lead to killing in the name of their religion; enslavement of people; superiority of one religion over another; and, government taking advantage of these differences all in the name of God. Let's get something perfectly clear, *God does not bless wars, or killing.* In fact, what is common among all religions is the "Golden Rule."

For example, Plato's Socrates states, "One should never do wrong in return, nor mistreat any man, nor matter, how one has been mistreated by him. (c. 469 BC – 399 BCE). Further back the Ancient Egyptian concept appearing in the story of The Eloquent Peasant (c. 2040 – 1650 BCE) says, "Now is the command: Do to the doer to cause that he do."

The Baháí Faith says, "Ascribe not to any soul that which wouldst not have ascribed to thee, and say not though doest not." Also, "Blessed is he who preferreth his brother before himself." Buddhists say, "Putting oneself in the place of another, one should not kill nor cause another to kill."

In Christianity, Luke 6:31 states "Do to others as you want them to do to you." While Muhammad, in the Farewell Sermon according to Islam said, "Hurt no one so that no one may hurt you." The Qur'ran also commends, "None of you [truly] believes until he wishes for his brother what he wishes for himself."

In Judaism (and Christianity's Old Testament), Leviticus 19:18 reads, "You shall not take vengeance or bear a grudge against your kinfolk. Love your neighbor as yourself. I am the LORD." Also in Leviticus 19:34, "The stranger who resides with you shall be to you as one of your citizens, you shall love him as yourself, for you were strangers in the land of Egypt: I am the LORD am your GOD."

In the Taoism, it states: "Regard your neighbor's gain as your own, and your neighbor's loss as your own loss."

In Hinduism, we read "One should never do that to another which one regards as injurious to one's own self.

This, in brief, is the rule of dharma. Other behavior is due to selfish desires." Humanism generally states the same principle: "do not treat people in a way you would not wish to be treated yourself."

The Golden Rule can best be summed up in one powerful word – *LOVE*. Jesus passed a commandment to his disciples – one that has often been ignored throughout centuries by man. It is best said in John 13:34, *"I give you a new commandment, that you love one another. Just as I have loved you, you should also love one another."* Ignored countless times in history, especially by Christians, electors, and appointees in government and leadership positions by examples of killing through wars, weapons of mass destruction, assassination plots, covert operations, oppression of people, enslavement of people, starvation, hunger, and homelessness. Yet, our "leaders" appear so "holy" as if they have not sinned by attending worship services seeking forgiveness for their trespasses repeatedly. Do you think God has not taken notice of these repeated and frequent transgressions? Of course, to Christianity, Jesus had died for our sins. But, don't you think this is pushing the limits just a little too far?

The other commonality in these religions is the source of inspiration for the Golden Rule – a higher source. Although it has yet to be proved, I believe God has manifested himself in each of the world's religions at different times of Earth's history and in such a manner as to express the Universal Truth of Love in the language understandable to the particular culture of the time. Therefore, He has made His presence known not only through Christ Jesus, but also through Abraham, Mohammed, Gautama Buddha, Lao Tzu, Dalai Lama, George Fox, Mother Ann Lee, John Thomas, and all the other religious founders of the world.

Even in today's world, a new spirituality movement is leading people in every nation to question their current religious beliefs. Individuals are being moved towards becoming one with the world. Is this an inspiration of God? Or, is this being driven by technology and social networking? Will governments around the world make attempts to shut down this migration of, perhaps, tearing down barriers that separate nations? Look at what companies like Facebook, Twitter and MySpace have done. They have literally brought people around the world closer and enabled them to communicate in any time zone, in real time. They have made the world much smaller. And, the trend continues. Yet, on the other hand, computerization has created impersonal, virtual relationships. Instead of direct physical and personal relationships and contacts, many friendships are made behind the walls and barriers of mechanized machines such as computers, tablets, and smartphones. This trend also needs to be addressed. People need more direct and personal contact with each other, especially if the world is to move in the right direction.

Historically, people have been conditioned to believe that we were always separate from God and isolated from the rest of the world. This is why man has created borders between nations; armies to defend their borders; and often led people to believe that we are disconnected from Earth's elements. Humans were typically put on "pedestals" as if we were a special creature of this planet with special God-given privileges and dominion over resources of this planet. Unfortunately, man has abused those privileges, and rather than being good a steward of the resources, he has abused, mismanaged and raped God's resources and all He has provided -- especially, in industrial countries where waste and pollution are particularly common all for the sake of profit. Man has greedily taken from the planet and has not replenished its resources. Nor has he had the foresight to make provisions to provide for suitable alternative resources. Existing resources are being quickly depleted while politics stand in the way of quickly finding suitable replacements (e.g. sustainable energy). But, I talk not only of energy issues, there are other issues with the Creator such as man's causing the extinction of many wildlife species which once roamed the Earth freely and many which are on the verge of extinction. Some species of whales, for example, are now extinct, because of man's over-zealousness for whaling.

If mankind is to survive as well as this Earth, humans must shed their belief in separation and superiority and realize that they are interconnected with everything on Earth as well as in this Universe. All life forms are dependent on each other for survival. There must be balance in life. Man has caused the greatest imbalance of life on Earth. He not only destroys himself, but all life forms around him: other animals, marine life, insects, and vegetation alike.

For example, following the Tohoku earthquake and tsunami near Fukushima, Japan, a great nuclear disaster occurred at the electric generating plant in that city. The disaster spilled nuclear waste into the ocean waters. While the public was led to believe that everything was under control and "safe," years later, it was discovered that Bluefin tuna caught off the shores of Southern California were all radioactive. The nuclear waste were ingested by the tuna while swimming off the coast of Fukushima. [iii] Some of the flesh of the tuna caught off shore may have found its way to sushi and seafood restaurants in the United States.

The Truth will manifest itself once again on Earth. But will man learn his lessons from the past and finally abide by the Truth? Or, will he live by his old habits and add, once again, his own interpretations and variances to the Truth and drift into violence, mistrust, and separation?

CHAPTER 2
HISTORY OF RELIGION
IT'S INFLUENCE ON GENERATIONS

Why then, do religions experience or encounter disharmony and conflicts if there are commonalities? Because with the growth of each religion come ritual practices, doctrines, cultural temperaments, and different traditions. All of which have distorted the essence, true meaning and intent of the philosophy. Along with the disharmony and conflicts, there have been splinter groups where religious groups could not come to agreement, so they subdivided into separate entities. Christianity is a prime example of this that can be traced back to its very inception in 325 AD.

I'm not going to focus on the Old Testament of the Bible as much as the New Testament. In 325 AD, the first New Testament of the Bible was produced after, presumably, several iterations and scholarly studies of scripture of various texts from various scrolls that were available to King Constantine's court during that time. Many things have been left out. Exactly what was important and what was not remains to be seen. I haven't been around those times to tell you. Nor am I a biblical scholar to say exactly what should have been included and so forth. But from a skeptic's point of view, there is controversy that surrounds the editorial stages of the New Testament. To simplify matters, there was a person by the name of Eusebius, a historian, who according to some stories, was a liar whom set up Christianity as a great hoax. I am not one to make judgment, but some of the behavior of the church leads me to believe that this may have been the case. Or, perhaps, ritual and doctrine, just so happened to interfere with the Truth of God -- *love.*

Regardless of what has happened in Christianity's beginnings, the Bible has had a tremendous influence on culture and society. Some have literally claimed it to be superior to the laws of their lands. Parts of the Bible have literally been taken out of context just for the sake of serving individual's wants and desires while ignoring the full verse that neighbors its passage or quotation. However, the Bible is not the only religious canon that has prevailed and influenced civic policies in the world. Other religious canons have also had a major influence in national policies and legislation as well.

Others, meanwhile, claim that the Bible reveals the future events of Earth through prophecy and selected text. Yet, the Bible has also been used in harmful ways such as giving people a "license" to kill, just because there are instances were tribes and groups of people having gone to war to defend their lands in the name of God. A good example of this are the Crusades in Europe where Christians fought Muslims over sacred lands. Soldiers were asked to lay down their lives for the sake of their rulers all in the name of a "higher calling." In actuality, there was no higher calling – it was in pure greed and hunger for power and the thrill of conquest over another people. However, to be fair, adherents of other religious faiths have also interpreted their beliefs that they too also have been given the "license" to kill also. In short, every religion in the world has swayed from the basic golden rule: "Do to others as you want them to do to you." All, in their own way have added "extra luggage" to this simple rule.

Man's conflict with himself and others are clearly explained in an article by Rod Cenzon entitled, "What is the Role of Reiyukai in Your Life?"

"We have seen how painfully man struggles for existence. He literally fights his way to the top. He has to assert himself. Ultimately, he suffers the consequences of his own actions. In the struggle self-assertion, in the struggle for power, in the struggle to possess and in the struggle to defend his own interests, there is always that inseparable partner – pain. He can't seem to get away from suffering. His egocentric tendencies have trapped him. So he finds himself constantly in conflict with himself and with others."[iv]

The saviors of the world have taught us God's Universal Love – both Christ Jesus and Gautama Buddha. Essentially what all religions, in their purity, teach is that in order to solve the world's problems of conflict and disharmony, we should learn the values of universal love. Christ has taught us this through his life and so have other masters of the World. We have contemporary masters such as His Holiness, the Dalai Lama and the Reverend Bishop Tutu. Unfortunately, these masters are being worshipped, while the practices and teachings are often being ignored.

To Christians, Jesus is the only Savior of the World. But, don't tell that to Buddhists or people in other religions. They will not accept that claim. The Jewish world is still waiting for their Messiah, others refer to Him as the Maitreya – The World Teacher. Many Christians today are waiting for His second coming.

Can it be that He has already come before, many years ago? Or can it be that he is with us now? Yes, it is true that God works in mysterious ways. Could God send His Son back to Earth in the form of a woman; in the form of a homeless person? Jesus may not come in such glory as He did when He first came. He may come quietly by night. Yet, He may come with an army of angelic beings. If you want to know what I believe -- I think He will come again soon according to prophecy.

In the early days of the United States, the Bible was used as an educational text book when many children were home-schooled. Many were taught how to read and write from the Bible. This essentially was the standard of education in the pioneering days of America.

In the industrial era, the Bible was eventually phased out in public education as there was an emphasis to separate government-sponsored institutions (i.e. public schools) from religion. Eventually the Bible was kept in the home and excluded in public schools. Most religious instruction was either done at home or in churches during Sunday School. Still, the Bible, as well as other religious influences were very strong. As for religious instruction in America, in general, these moved out of the homes and schools and were mainly taught on Sundays or during weekday Bible studies. In some companies, small groups met during lunch periods for Bible and prayer sessions. In some countries, they are calls to prayer during the day and these are practiced in the work place as well. Many went to temples before and after work. In Muslim countries, the faithful pray five times a day.

But as new generations have come to pass, religious

influences have deteriorated dramatically. Other values that each generation perceived as more important, have supplanted the importance of religion. Ask a young person who some of the important people of the Bible are, and you might not get a response.

We cannot expect traditional beliefs, practices, and behaviors to live on forever. The world is constantly changing around us. God is forever in motion and is forever changing and making things for the better. Where we once held beliefs that were important to our ancestors and ourselves, they may not hold true for future generations to come. We may just be seeing this shift in our lives today. Hence, church attendance is declining across the board in all religions.

Do not be judgmental by automatically saying that something evil is taking place. It may very well be that we are seeing the manifestation of the Truth in a totally new form that will be understood by the younger generation, such as that which was passed along in Old Testament times, then in New Testament times, and so on. The evilness of this whole issue, as a matter of fact, started eons ago when the world decided to diminish the quality of education by eliminating religion and arts in schools – especially in nations where testing of basics became more important rather than the overall balanced, well-rounded education of a child -- where passing standardized exams became more important over critical thinking. I'll talk about this subject more in a chapter of itself.

Many young adults were educated at home by their parents or grandparents. Students are provided more freedom to accelerate on their own. This simple educational process often included some form of lessons in art – writing or music. Students were better taught the art and skill of penmanship and a better understanding of their respective language. This was common across all religions of the world. There was a pitfall in this process, however. Frequently, personal biases would influence the educational process during these times. Sometimes for the good, sometimes home schooling had underscored separation and isolation. This has manifested itself through some generations. Unfortunately, the world has suffered the consequences of some of these "home grown" teachings. This has separated peoples of the world from better understanding each other. It has created a deeper division between religions and their followers seeding mistrust among nations resulting in war.

The pendulum swings throughout time – extremely in one direction, yet enormously in the opposite direction. Some in this world are hoping that the pendulum will sway in the direction when religion will be totally abandoned in the world in order to establish total control and dominance by creating a one world order ruled by one or two-percent of the world's population. To avoid this, the people of the world must unite and grasp power as one voice while still maintaining our spiritual beliefs. However we must shed our dogmas and return to the basics. I will explain how to do this in subsequent chapters.

Throughout history, there have been many positive contributions of religion to humanity. Yet, on the other hand, there have been many negative aspects about religion which have turned many people off. In some cases, it has inhibited progress – especially in the realm of science. Some religious groups have influenced their governments to pass legislation limiting science to further explore and offer enhancements to mankind. Many have claimed that it wasn't in God's "plans."

Everything is inspired by God. We have all been given unique gifts and talents. Who is not to say that God hasn't given certain people the keys (gifts and talents) of scientific discovery -- the gift of maintaining life like "automobile mechanics?" Has anyone thought that stem cell research might be God's answer to solving a lot of our medical problems? Could this be His away of updating his "maintenance manual" for us? Many people in the world have also benefitted from medical advancements made by way of organ transplants as well. We have become so accustomed to our rituals and traditions, that we have not allowed God to make major changes in our lives. New and exciting things are awaiting to happen. Much of it can benefit and enhance life. However, in order for these changes to happen, we need to open our minds and accept what God has to offer – not shut them out because of our fears or our ways of living habitually.

Through our historically habitual ways of living, we have developed contradictory attitudes about the values of life as well. Many people say that life is valuable. This is true. But what is contradictory in the argument is that some life is more valuable than others. Some people believe that human life, although not yet born, is more valuable than human life already living. That is, we take extraordinary measures, including legislation that will save an unborn fetus while, in the process, existing life forms may be expendable for the sacrifice of these unborn children. Such as, prohibiting or limiting the research of stem cells which may cure cancer and other ailments and save lives of many living people. Yet, these potential people have to be sacrificed in order to save the future of those yet to be born. Yet, they argue that "life *is* valuable." To God, *all* life is precious. He has answers to preserving *all* life forms, not just a select few. However, if man has already found a way to eliminate a lot of species from the face of this planet, he has already learned to limit the resources to his own kind. Therefore, he will devise a way to eliminate and reduce his own species if allowed to do so. And, according to some circles, there are plans on the drawing boards to do just that.[v]

Masters and teachers who have brought the truth to the world have often been chastised. Even put to death in earlier centuries. In modern times, if their views do not conform to religious beliefs, they are often incarcerated in mental institutions – largely in an attempt to hide or subvert the truth. *The truth will set people free*. However, the Truth is disruptive to the process of mind control. If it is not religions playing having a part of this, government is also a major factor in this process. Man has always found a way of either hiding the truth or of disposing of the truth if it doesn't agree with him -- especially, when it often inconvenienced him, his ego and ambitions.

Some countries claim that they guarantee freedoms of expression and speech when, in actuality, these are only myths offset by contradictory practices and laws. God granted each individual free and independent thinking and creativity. Man has exerted his own rules and regulations that have negated this freedom. God works through every person and does not demand perfection. Man has persistently demanded perfection and has developed means of punishing those who do not meet those expectations. Such as, he has developed scoring systems in athletics or artistic achievement. When athletes or artists do not meet a level of perfection, they are graded down. Humans are not perfect beings – this is a physical law. Humans should not be judged or compared against each other, but individually by their own achievements.

Many times, people have a habit of overly criticizing others rather than looking at the positive merits of a person. Furthermore, they never offer constructive criticism, but only negative feedback. They have yet to learn and recognize the beauty in everything and there are positive elements in everything. However, they will not learn how to provide positive feedback unless they, too have learned that they are connected with everything in life. People have always had an inherent tendency of finding more fault in others rather than recognizing the positive contributions individuals have made. They are quick to blame, but often reluctant to give recognition. We must continually reinforce the positive merits of individuals and de-emphasize the faults.

In drawing this chapter to a close, I leave you with these famous words: *"United we stand, divided we fall."*[vi]

CHAPTER 3

APPLICATION OF DOCTRINES AND RELIGIOUS DOCUMENTS IN CONTEMPORARY TIMES

As with all other contemporary activities in today's modern world, religion will have to compete for peoples' time and money. This is why churches are experiencing dwindling attendances, not only in Christian churches – but across the board. This is not necessarily true for so called "mega churches," but on average, most congregations are struggling to survive. Many are closing their doors while others are merging with other ethnic denominations in order to keep revenues from decreasing.

Times have changed dramatically. No longer does the present generation consider church attendance on Sundays to be as important as with previous generations. Why? Have individual values changed? An excellent film by Dr. Morris Massey illustrates this phenomenon. This educational lecture is entitled, *What You Are Is What You Were When*, was produced was released in the 1970's and revised in 1986.

The film investigates the role of the past by explaining the three self-programming periods that each young individual goes through in developing a value system.

Each generation has a different set of values. There may be some overlap. Yet, peer influences will present totally different values within each generational set. For generations in the past, the Bible was held in high esteem. That is not so in today's world where people could barely read the newspapers, let alone the Bible – nor can they point on the map where their native country is in the world. Our educational system has decayed dramatically. Newer generations care, if it is important to them and the values that are important to them. What Baby Boomers value is not valued by generations that follow. The strategies used by evangelists that once were successful in reaching out to unbelievers, are no longer applicable in today's society. You cannot simply force your values and beliefs on the new generation using old, once proven tactics -- especially in a world where spiritual values in the world are changing dramatically. Rather being divided between religious values and beliefs, and increasing number of people are shedding traditional beliefs which have often separated us, and are moving towards global oneness. Not in the direction of a "one-world order" which some theorize is going to occur, but a spiritual movement that is more powerful than powers on this planet. It's safe to say that there is a new spiritual migration that is operating on "multi-levels."

Here is how traditionalists fail to communicate with new generations. To Buddhists, "Nirvana" is like Heaven to Christians. The newer generations would consider Nirvana as a "classic oldies station or the famous rock group."[vii] Whereas older generations would consider great artists as Beethoven, the composer, and Michelangelo, the painter/

sculptor – the newer generation would think of Beethoven as a dog and Michelangelo as a computer virus. Truly, there is a generational disconnect. So, if you try to speak to the new generations using biblical language and phrases out of traditional doctrines and documents, you may be attempting to communicate to them in a "foreign" language.

So, will the Bible be applicable in the future? A lot of good things have been written in the Bible. That said, the Bible, for example -- in reality -- has created divisions within Christianity ever since its creation. Just how much of it was actually the "Word of God" and how much was tainted by man in order to control mankind? I can safely say this about doctrines of other religions: they have all departed from the Golden Rule and have instead built in rituals and traditions that have caused disagreements within their respective religions, violence, and even wars. We have all become so accustomed to the traditions and values of our respective religions that if we even depart from traditional thinking or from the norm, we are excommunicated and hence, marked for life. And, this is a total deviation of what our masters have taught – forgiveness. Instead of valuing love and forgiveness, we practice and worship hatred and violence. We are constantly living in fear rather than letting the power of love, understanding, tolerance, and acceptance to overcome our fearful behavior and paranoia. In many countries, they call themselves "peace loving nations" while considering themselves as "warriors." You cannot have it both ways.

So, getting back to the question: Will the Bible be relevant in the future? Perhaps very little of it – but, this also holds true for other religions as well. Old traditions, practices and rituals will have to be shed. It's like preparing to go on a very long journey – you need to travel light. So must you clear you mind of all the clutter and things that weigh you down. A lot of things that you have learned in your religions have weighed you down to the point where mankind cannot progress – but is constantly living in the past, with past traditions and practices. Time moves forward. Therefore, time and progress will move with or without you – it's your choice.

Thousands of years passed between the Old Testament and the New Testament. Don't be surprised to learn that an updated Testament is yet to come – one that will shed old traditions, practices, ideologies and beliefs, and moves people towards nonviolence, love, forgiveness, harmony and oneness in the world – a universal testament that will bring people of the world together.

Doctrines and religious teachings have been used to separate man from the ultimate universal truth by substituting man's own interpretations of the real truth in order to control minds of people --therefore, creating institutional rituals and beliefs that were worshipped rather than practicing the true spirit of the message. Where masters such as Jesus Christ, and the Buddha, differently interpreted by people many years after, some of which were distorted causing divisions among different religions and various branches thereof. Man has been conditioned to think that we were always separate from our Creator or a higher being. We were always told to look elsewhere for our spiritual guidance and counseling for it always came from somewhere else. Only very few religions have taught that God, the Creator, or the Supreme Being, was actually close at hand. So close that -- for the sake of referring this spirit as one -- God actually is a part of each individual. God actually resides in each human being and is a part of every creature on Earth. God is within us, among us, and all around us. It is through this that we are connected to everything and everything is connected to us as individuals. We are not separate from each other and from other life forms. Yet, because we still act and think we are separate from each other and from other things, man continues to destroy the world and other people. As I eluded to in my first book, *Kami Jin*, soon there will be no nations to destroy or conquer since humanity itself will have been destroyed by man himself.

When you are given a course of survival training at the Boy Scout Reservation in Philmont located at Cimarron, New Mexico, you are instructed to take only a spoon and leave behind the fork and knife. With a spoon, you can also cut as well as eat your meals with. This principle can also be applied to your spiritual travels – travel lightly and carry only what is essential for your journey. This means leaving your "survival books" behind. By living in the wilderness, God, your Creator, truly becomes your guide. You come to learn that you are connected with everything and experience the presence of God.

If mankind is to move in the right direction, then it will have to abandon all of its excess luggage and travel lightly with only the bare essentials. Only those who travel lightly will be able to move forward. Those who insist on carrying baggage will be left behind.

SECTION TWO

A HISTORY OF
PEOPLE CONTROL

CHAPTER 4
ANCIENT TIMES

Perhaps Earth's earliest, if not the most original form, of a computer memory system is the human brain. The brain has an amazing capacity of storing an enormous amount of memory and keeping it organized. Even today, it is still a wonder to medicine and scientists how the brain functions. But even so, the brain has a limited capacity for logic and reasoning. Therefore, man has invented computer systems to expand his capabilities. In many ways, it has benefited man. But to a certain degree, it has minimized his capacity to solve problems on his own by the mere fact that he has opted to delegate some of that power to the computer. For example, basic mathematical calculations have now become dependent on calculators and computers. A lot of humans have lost their capacity to perform such basic mathematical computations without such devices

Throughout history, man has always tried to control his own kind in some form or fashion using various approaches and techniques. The methods of controlling people have become more sophisticated through the progression of history. There have been so much written on the subject of mind control itself that all you have to do is enter the term in your favorite search engine and you will find multitudes of articles written on the subject. Some are neutral and unbiased, some are slanted with religious overtones.

Typically, there has always been one group or class of people influencing their domination over multitudes of others. What or who has made them so unique is anyone's guess --it probably started even before Biblical times. Why relatively very few people would claim superiority over the majority of the world's population is unknown. For sure, God has not granted them this esteemed status and dominion over others. After all, why can't they provide the papers written by Him that bestows these rights upon them? God has planned for all men to have equal rights and dominion over this Earth. He has not given special privileges to certain individuals or families. These rights were only bestowed by man and handed down through generations.

The aristocracy of the world has exerted their power to dictate the directions of mankind. Often, these decisions are not of God. Many are and have been sacrificed because of their desire to control the world by controlling and limiting resources, causing wars among nations for the sake of profits and personal gain. Yet, it is often the members of the underclass who have to do their fighting. Think about it – in ancient Rome, the rich often entertained themselves by going to the Coliseum to watch gladiators battle it out to the death. Or, in some cases, defend their lives before lions. In the Bible, there are numerous references to slavery illustrating the dominance of a certain elite group of people over the masses.

Various methods of controlling people were used: imprisonment, slavery, drugs, sorcery and witchcraft, and a variety of other means. But "mind control" doesn't necessarily have to be considered as only those which served evil and greedy purposes. Government, religion and education are also forms of controlling peoples' behavior, thought patterns, beliefs, and values. These three institutions alone have influenced the way peoples of the world learn about what is good, bad, what to learn about in schools, establishing values in their respective nations. Hence, we have cultural differences and beliefs. In some countries, there is a strong influence of religion in their governments.

Yet, in other countries, there is separation of church and state. Women in some countries are required to cover up entirely. And when visitors from these countries visit other, more liberal nations, they are shocked and offended when they see women wearing practically nothing on the beach.

Yes, there *is* a wide spectrum of beliefs and values. They are all right in their own respects, none are wrong. Not good, not bad. To God, there is no good nor bad, right nor wrong. These have been defined purely by man. So, it all depends on which party line you wish to follow. But the beliefs and values among factions are so strong that they separate people to the point where violent disagreements have erupted causing wars in the name of their religions. Millions of men, women and children died, all because political and religious leaders could not learn how to respect each other's opposing values and way of life. Rather than "let each other be, peacefully" there is and always has been the imposition of one's beliefs over another. One's values were always greater than the other even to the point of fighting over. We have seen this not only in crusades, but in prehistoric man's history, in world wars, and every conflict on Earth. Although man has made many impressive advances since the pre-historic times, he has yet to evolve to a higher level of civilized thinking where he can fully live peacefully among fellow men.

CHAPTER 5
PRE-INDUSTRIAL

A LOOK AT SLAVERY

History has recorded at least two major instances where man has dominated his own kind in the form of slavery. The first major example was the enslavement of the Israelites under Pharaoh. The second illustration was the enslavement of Africans in America to colonists of the new world. There are countless others which have not been recorded in history. A lot of examples appear in current news -- such as, human trafficking of sex slaves and prostitutes, abduction of infants and children, familial imprisonment and incarceration.

In educational systems, there were differences in the quality of education offered to different races and nationalities. Some were provided better education than others – hence, there was a wide discrepancy among nations. The discrepancies exist even today. Many are educated to think they are still superior to others and often behave as such. Man has yet to equalize the playing field. And for as long as this superiority mentality exists, he probably never will try to equalize the playing field.

Slavery is one example of how elite classes of men have exerted their powers over multitudes of fellow humans. In fact, these two examples illustrate how one race had dominated their influence over another – one thinking that they were superior over the other. Ironically, in the case of American slavery, it was written that "*all men were created equal.*" Still, the struggles for equality exist even in contemporary times. An elite class of people continues to wield their influence in companies and government. As children, we have always been taught to go to school and study hard, then continue on to college and get a good education so that we can make a good living and advance in life. This was the "American Dream." But dreams were often shattered when young adults discovered after graduating from college that they really couldn't move up the ladder without "playing the game of corporate politics." Many people already at the top didn't even have a college education, let alone being high school drop-outs themselves. No matter where one turned, whether it seemed like an honest business or not, they were all a "*pyramid scheme.*" There was really no way of moving up the ladder – it was all an illusion reserved for a chosen few.

In America, there are two classic ways to illustrate this point. The first is the military. There are the officers who are paid quite well and have very nice retirement benefits. Then, there are the enlisted personnel, or those in the lower ranks who have good benefits as long as they are serving. These people are often on the front lines putting their lives in jeopardy while the officers are in the rear living in luxury. Yet, the front line personnel are highly expendable – not only with their lives, but when they leave the service, many of them often do not have job to return to and often become homeless with very little assistance. This is the lack of respect from society after serving their country and being asked to sacrifice their lives all for the sake of the nation's security. Yet, the nation cannot manage to provide them with affordable living accommodations, health care, nor transition them back into a normal civilian life after serving their country.

Then the second example is employees of large corporations. Executives are paid exceeding well while their employees on the front lines are paid paltry wages. Sure, executives will say they (employees) are paid "fairly." But exactly what is fair? Frontline employees often struggle to make ends meet because of inflation and inadequate wages or salaries. It is a continuous struggle. Executives, on the other hand, are being paid millions, if not billions of dollars annually and do not even have a clue as to the real struggles of the working class. This habit of paying workers pennies while the master keeps the bulk of the profits can be traced back to ancient times. The concept is no different – just multiplied by millions.

A classic example of this are American corporations who find it difficult to pay their first-line employees a "living minimum wage" while rewarding their corporate executives a more than generous annual salary and bonus.

Then, when it comes to downsizing, it is often the working employees who are expendable. How hypocritical can executives be? They label their employees the most valuable assets of their companies while laying them off, then in return, they (the executives) reward themselves with millions of dollars in bonuses just for putting people out of their jobs! And, they continue to feast and dine in luxury. They export jobs overseas while government does absolutely nothing to protect the jobs and lives of the citizens that elected them into office.

For ages, mankind has always lived by the "trickle down" concept. Unfortunately, the fat cat has become even sinfully bloated while many in the world are suffering starvation and homelessness. Governments, heavily influenced by the wealthy often sway their policies and legislations benefitting those with money giving very little voice to those who are less fortunate and for the populace whom have placed their trust in elected officials. Modern-day politics has become tainted with corruption. Very few politicians practice high ethical standards by keeping the faith of the people and serving them rather than special interests.

Is there the slightest trace of honesty on Earth anymore? Practically everything that you look at resembles the form of a "pyramid." Is this coincidental or by design? Or, is this all that mankind knows? Think about it. There are governments at all levels, corporations large and small. Even in the private sector, there are your online money-making schemes like multiple-level-marketing scams that are out for all the money you have -- many which the government considers as corrupt and illegal. But in actuality, what is not corrupt? If you really look at the behavior these activities, they all have a degree of corruption that does not serve mankind well.

God has called upon certain individuals to lead by wisdom and example. They were true leaders of their people -- ones that could be respected such as Abraham and Moses. Jesus and Mohammed were also undeniably great leaders as well. In Asia, Buddha and Confucius also influenced the multitudes. All of these examples were great not because they were wealthy, nor placed themselves on a pedestal. They were humble servants of the people. Unlike in today's world where greed and materialism are dominant characteristics of self-proclaimed leaders of the world, the great leaders of history were teachers, masters of imparting truth and wisdom. Very few individuals do this in today's world. However, they are overshadowed by corporate executives and government officials that are often not out for the best interest of the people.

For too long in the history of mankind, people have always yielded to the powers and influences of those individuals and groups of people with controlling personality disorders. It was and still is an epidemic that mandates a cure. People with controlling personalities often struggle with superiority. This trait is often found in people with vast amounts of wealth, politics, and company leadership. Society still has not found a way to confront these people effectively but more, or less, has tolerated their behavior. Unfortunately, their behavior has become uncontrollable and unmanageable. Greed has become a symptom of this worsening illness that has infected many people with this kind of personality. Many people have suffered because of their behavior either it be psychologically, physically, verbally, or a combination of all three. *Controlling Personality Syndrome is nothing new.* This illness has existed since the beginning of mankind. There always has been at least one who has always tried to dominate and exert his powers and influence over the tribe. When someone challenged his "authority," there were often battles to the death. In modern days, the illness has become even more serious. It often involves a lot of money, reputation, and also can result in homicide or a case of physical misfortune.

In many ways, although it may appear that man is sophisticated to some degree through the advent of time, his mind and behavior is still very primitive. This is one thing that has yet to evolve to a higher degree of civilized intelligence.

Man must learn new intellectual levels of programming and must have the freedom to explore new concepts and ideas without being inhibited by other influences trying to control the populous minds through propaganda, "standardized" education by a nation which has established different standards for different classes of people, drug induced influences, and other forced ways of creating a society of "human robots or clones." As in computer programming, there should be a basic core curriculum of educating humans adapted by the world – not only by singular nations. But by and large, the education of individuals should be tailored to cognitive learning preferences in order to achieve the highest degree of educational success for the individual. Many countries force children through an "educational assembly line." Children are processed through school systems without having learned, nor mastered a single subject. There is more emphasis on testing rather than establishing student-teacher relationships or, mentors. And because the illness of controlling personalities has become so unmanageable in society, we have become immune and tolerant to the phenomena of "bullying" in schools at all levels. Yes, school officials recognize that bullying exists in schools, but rarely discipline the students who are guilty of such despicable behavior. Ironically, it's the victims of bullying that suffer the consequences -- sometimes paid for with their lives. Are school systems reinforcing the development of future bullies? Is society becoming so numb that life is no longer important or valuable even when a victim of bullying takes his or her life? Yet, we take no action to correct the problem itself.

In some cultures, controlling personalities are often reinforced by customs and traditions. Take for the example of the role of men being dominant over women. Wives are expected to be submissive to their husbands. It's not an equal relationship as in Western cultures, but the husband has the predominant role in the family as head of household. He is responsible for making all decisions. In Western society, it is typically more equal even though the man had the more dominant role. In some families, it's equal. Yet, in present day, there are instances where the wife plays the greater role as bread winner since the husband is unemployed.

But in some cases, where the male dominance is challenged by the female, familial disputes result. Occasionally in physical harm, sometimes it is so serious that it cost the wife or the mother her life. Then too, sometimes the husband winds up dead as well. All because of the struggle for control – especially during divorce proceedings where there are custody battles between couples over children. This often has damaging long-term effects on the offspring later on in adulthood. Sometimes, the mental scars are so serious that the adolescents never get over it.

If the world is to change, people must learn how to effectively confront those with controlling personalities. People with these disorders need the services of a therapist, for they affect the lives, health and well-being of others as well. And the most unfortunate thing about this is that they are totally unaware they causing these problems – in total denial. In the work place, people with these personalities cause a high rate of stress, anxiety, hypertension, and cardiac disorders. If the behavior is bad enough, employees or subordinates who cannot tolerate their behavior often react negatively with opposing actions, sometimes causing physical harm and violence.

There are many people with these disorders in high positions of authority. However, there are even more individuals in the world that are rational, who can resist this behavior and eventually put people like these in their proper place in the world. We should not tolerate, nor let people with controlling personalities continue to control our lives, nor dictate our way of living – especially if it appears that their leadership is taking the nation or the world in the wrong direction. People should educate themselves to recognize the traits and characteristics of controlling personalities and defend against their domineering influence. All it takes is just one word: "*No!*"

The famous French author Albert Camus once said, "Don't walk in front of me; I may not follow. Don't walk behind me; I may not lead. Just walk beside me and be my friend." In all of our relationships, weather in the workplace in in family life, we should neither take the lead, nor follow. But walk or travel through this journey of life together as "friends."

Even to this day, society still retains that "master-slave" mentality through government, industry, and education. This will not serve mankind well as humanity strives to move forward in the right direction. Mankind must find a way of seeing, working with, and treating everyone as "equals."

CHAPTER 6
INDUSTRIAL

L et's jump several centuries into the present. Man's quest to control the minds of people has not changed, but interestingly, has been amplified with the advent of new tools offered with the advancement of technology starting in the industrial age. In fact, his ambitions of doing so have become even more sinister as he has advanced his techniques. Let's examine a few ways he has done so.

PROPAGANDA AND FALSE INFORMATION

One of the most effective techniques governments used to control its "sheep" or citizens was to use propaganda and disinformation -- especially when it needed to conceal the truth. Agencies would be notorious for covering up the facts by using their own "experts" to fabricate or distort the facts, present false evidence and often go on campaigns to disprove other notable experts in the field as wrong. They were masters of creating doubt which often led to debate and argument. Often, false or fabricated facts were used as an excuse to declare war against another country. The people of the country were not informed of the real motives for going to war. The truth was that a lot of innocent people were sacrificed and slaughtered because of lies and misinformation. But, the citizens, with their unwavering faith in government, swallowed the bait, hook, line, and sinker. There was no way out. Many innocent sons and daughters were asked to place their lives on the line for a government that trumped up the necessity to go to war -- for what? Yet in return, there were no plans to transition these of service members back into society. Many returned to their countries without proper medical care and a home to return to. Yet, many people felt that the country owed them nothing for their service. Are some nations filled with ungrateful leaders only looking out for themselves and their own greedy agenda? Are the people of the countries being used as pawns for a more sinister plot? Let's look another way these people are using another tool to control the populous.

ADVERTISING

The development of technology has been both a blessing and a diabolical curse. Many things like television, radio, computer, and cell phones have made communications much easier. In many ways, they have brought the world much closer – especially with the advent of the Internet. However, it is a diabolical curse because it has diminished personal relationships – the ability to better communicate and establish relationships one-to-one and, even more importantly, more directly in a personal way. The "physical touch" has disappeared.

With this technology, negative forces and influences have also taken advantage of these devices to promote their message of false and misleading information. Take advertising for example. A lot of advertising messages aren't really about the product, but are meant to sell an idea. Typically, they are targeting the subliminal mind. Or, in other words, it is an attempt of hypnosis over the air waves. If you are sold on an idea or remember the message, you would go out and buy the product – whether you needed it or not. The product may even be bad for your health. But you were sold on the idea that it was "good" for your health. Without doing any research on the product, you trusted the message – the advertisement. In other words, you were "hooked."

An example of this is the way the military advertises for their recruits. They advertise a glorious, honorable life of service. But when you enlist and begin service, it is actually a totally different experience –a prime example of misleading advertising.

Politicians during elections are notorious for false advertising. They typically make campaign promises they never keep. That's because once they get into office, the political environment is so radically different in reality, it is impossible to keep promises they make. The opposition in government is always stronger than during the campaign. The test of any politician is, how well will they actually fare in government? Experience has absolutely no basis for running for office. Qualifications are important. But more importantly, is the person focused on his constituency, or is this individual easily influenced by special interest groups? The candidate's history and behavior matter as well has integrity and ethical standards. Furthermore, does the politician offer solutions instead of slinging mud at the other candidate? Is he or she more focused on his or her own campaign and merits rather than running in paranoia and fear of losing to the other candidates?

DECEPTION

No matter where you look or where you go, you encounter some degree of deception just about everywhere. The word "deception" is a very broad term for deceiving and controlling people's minds. Let's look at some synonyms that may fit some other people better: artifice, cheating, cozenage, craft, craftiness, crookedness, cunning, deceitfulness, deceit, deceptiveness, deception, dishonesty, dissembling, dissimulation, double-dealing, dupery, duplicity, fakery, foxiness, fraud, guile, guilefulness, wile.

Such characteristics of people were quite common, not only in present day, but also in ancient Biblical times like in the days of Sodom and Gomorrah. The same things that drove people of back then, drive the same types of people of today, evil, lust, an insatiable greed and love for money. You would think that after a city has been demolished by God that man would have learned his lessons though time. Obviously, this has not happened. We have yet to develop a more sophisticated level of thinking.

Many people, especially in government and business, continue to deceive people though cheating, craftiness, cunningness, deceit, double-dealing, and duplicity. Fraud has become a commonality and an epidemic. Yet, the people of the world continue to tolerate this behavior. For the world to move forward, these behaviors must be corrected and must become intolerable in a sophisticated society of higher thinking.

UNRESPONSIVE GOVERNMENT

It would almost appear that with each passing day, government becomes more unresponsive to the people. Of course, officials say they are trying their best to serve the people. But truthfully, their backroom dealings with lobbyists and special interest groups are not serving the people at all. The people who elected them to serve are not being represented at all. Just follow the money and its influence on your elected representatives. Your elected representatives are actually responsive to the people and interests who contributed to their coffers, not those who voted for them at the ballot boxes. And many of the special interests and lobbyists do not even reside in the representative's own district. Corruption has flooded the halls of government all over the world. Man thinks this is not noticed elsewhere, but it is being noticed in Heaven and in other parts of the Universe.

Evilness and corruption have also infiltrated churches as well. Many people have become so engulfed in politics and money that they have totally lost their true mission and focus for caring for people and their needs, the community, and the world. Many of you have adapted the selfish "what's in it for me?" attitude. Rather than "what's in it for us?" or "How can I help you?" You have placed yourselves on pedestals. In some countries, you have come to think that you are far superior then everyone else in the world. Yet, you forget that there are many starving and homeless. Yet, you care nothing about them. You have become nations and people of profit and have lost your sense of true service to others. Yes, you say you serve others some times. But this is not good enough -- it is only a token amount. If you truly served others diligently as in service to God, there would be no poverty, starvation, nor homelessness. But the leaders of your churches enrich themselves with vast amounts of money from their congregations in mega churches rather than channeling the money to support the poor – especially in times of economic hardship. You lavish yourselves with fancy material luxuries, while many find it difficult to even buy a cup of coffee. These people try to find comfort on park benches, parking lots of parks and beaches, benches and walk ways of churches and synagogues. Yet, you will have no part of them. You have forced them out of their homes, taken away their credit and money, and have made life difficult for them to return back to society by creating inhumane credit records and databases which follow them for the remainder of their lives. Yet, you grant special privileges to the corrupted people of the world by granting them unlimited access to the wealth and resources of the Earth. You have not learned to share the Earth's resources but have acted as selfish children. The cries of these people are being heard in Heaven.

CORPORATE AND GOVERNMENT CONTROL OF PRESS AND MEDIA

There used to be a time when journalists were independent, free to report on news and events without being influenced and dictated to by government and/or corporate leaders. Times have changed and it's all in the spirit of controlling people's minds.

One way of doing this is to "spoon feed" what is said

over the air waves on television and radio. No longer are news bureaus free to cover what is truly important, but what is important to corporate executives and government. There used to be a concept of "freedom of speech and expression," and freedom of press -- that has all eroded away and are only words on paper. News is now censored by corporations and government. Journalists are no longer free to report on the news realistically.

During the Iraq War, government forbid news agencies from publishing photos of coffins returning from war, draped with American Flags. Apparently, the government did not want the public to know that there were heavy casualties during the war. It wanted the public to know that casualties were at a minimum, rather than being realistic --a government practicing the art of deception against its own people.

GOVERNMENT CORRUPTION AND CORPORATE LOBBYISTS

I've already said a few things about corruption in government, corporate lobbyists and special interest groups already. Since it is know that they have already tainted government already, it is not worth repeating it again. However, government officials should be expected to fulfill their positions with levels of high integrity and ethical standards. Unfortunately, many of them have accepted bribes and special interest money from contributors who have often influenced their legislative behavior. In many ways, not in favor of their constituents, but in favor a minority who have bought off government. Even more so, they have influenced the way that judges make decisions on high courts.

The Federal Government was designed as a democracy to serve the people of the country – not for corporations. In the Constitution, it says a "Government by the people, and for the people…" However, the Supreme Court decided that corporations are "people" too.[viii] This is a mistake. The executives who run the corporations have been granted equal rights by the Courts as people of the country – no more, no less. The average person in America was also guaranteed the same rights. However, the balance has shifted when executives were given more rights, a bigger voice in government as a collective "people." This, however, is not recognized in the Constitution and never was intended to be granted to corporations. But money has influenced the decision and policy making behavior of legislators and adjudicators in government. It is no longer a government by the "people and for the people." It is more a "government for corporations, by corporations."

The Supreme Court decision gave corporations the freedom to "buy" elections or heavily influence the outcome of an election by endorsing candidates of their choice though advertising. This is not what the Founding fathers had designed for the country. They intended fair, democratic elections. Recently, elections have become tainted with scandals and questionable practices by political parties.

Furthermore, the founders of this country designed the government to be run by three branches of the Federal Government – the Executive Branch, Legislative and Judicial Branches. There were checks and balances built into the system. However, with corporate influences corrupting all three branches of the federal government, there are no checks and balances left.

In addition, the government never was designed to be controlled by a higher secretive circle of world bankers who dictate the direction of the nation's economy and behavior of the federal government. The federal government is, more or less, a puppet to this elite organization of world leaders and bankers attempting to establish a one world order. Presidents and world leaders have been assassinated because they refused to adhere to the mandates of this secretive group of people.

If man is to move forward in the right direction, the people of the world will have to rise up against these secretive groups. The world can no longer afford to tolerate these dictators that inhibit the progress of mankind and work against the will of God. They must be exposed and brought to justice.

IMPRISONMENT, ENSLAVEMENT, TORTURE, AND TECHNOLOGY

Governments have also used other methods to force people to change their minds unwillingly though methods of enslavement, imprisonment, torture, and technological devices.

During battles, prisoners of war would often be tortured while imprisoned in order to obtain strategic information about the opposition. Many of these techniques and practices were often ineffective and useless, but often resulted in permanent psychological damage to the individual. In modern times, some prisoners were implanted with electronic devices in order to manipulate their thought processes.[ix] This was occurring in countries where they were known for identifying inhumane practices in other countries, yet, they carried out dastardly atrocities themselves and covered it up, then claimed that international law never applied to them.

In many ways, technology has served mankind well. However, man has also discovered ways to use technology for sinister purposes. Take the microwave for example. Wonderful things can be done with microwave technology such as cooking and transmitting voice over the air waves. There are many installations that cause this to happen. Yet, some studies have also shown that this technology can be harmful to one's health as well. Cell phones, for example, have mobilized telecommunications and the Internet. Yet, the prolonged use of cell phones can damage one's hearing.

The use of microwaves can also be used for other means of hidden communication such as broadcasting subliminal messages out to the populous. The human body is constantly being bombarded with radio waves passing through each body daily. One form of controlling the masses would be to send signals out via radio waves (microwaves) to control people's minds. And, if each person were to be implanted with an electronic receptor, they would be able to do this even more effectively. Especially if the implant was designed to electronically alter the brain's behavior instantaneously.[x]

CHAPTER 7
IMMEDIATE FUTURE

In order for mankind to move forward, we must clear a lot of obstacles. First and foremost, we must abandon the practice of treating and controlling people as "puppets." Human beings were given the ability of free thinking and expression, and to travel freely. Man has always tried ways to "bottle" or "contain" this freedom by various methods such as:

- Governments
- Borders
- Slavery (of people and nations)
- Unequal monetary systems
- Limiting/Restricting Resources
- Restricting or Limiting Travel
- Creating different levels (quality) of educational systems
- Social classes
- Religious doctrines
- Censorship
- Police State

Although the role of a government is essential in any civilization, one must consider the honesty and integrity of its leaders. A form of government without high ethical standards does not serve its citizens well. This is evidenced by the deterioration within the walls of government. Elected officials are corrupted not only by their legislative practices, but also are found to be highly susceptible of other behavior not favorable in the eyes of the public.

Follow the money trail even higher and one may discover that its own government is a puppet to other influential entities that may not have the best interest of the people at hand. Moreover, the agenda of this small group of people may have global designs for even greater destruction of a nation or a multitude of countries. The world needs to wake up and pay close attention to the behavior and actions of its leaders. Governments have been notorious for practicing deception on its people. Even the ones that appear to be "honest" or "transparent" are just as at fault. In fact, for those who say that there needs to be more transparency in government, be wary and skeptical. In all likelihood, there is a hidden agenda.[xi]

The world's currency system has been used to limit the vast amount of resources available to mankind. And, the intent of limiting these resources has not been in the act of good stewardship or management of Earth's resources. The purposes of limiting resources were for greed – profit. If supplies were low, the cost was intentionally inflated. The more plentiful the supply, the less amount of profit was available to business. As the world progressed through time, the resources were "masterfully" dwindled to cause inflationary periods of history. But the profits did not trickle down to the common man. Most of the pot went to those whom were already well off.

During the recession in the 21st Century, many companies in the United States went bankrupt. To save these major corporations, the government stepped in with "bailout" money. Rather than let these companies go down in history and move towards building the future, the government elected to save these entities of the past by printing more money backed by nothing but worthless data in a computer system – most of "money" rewarded corporate executives for bad management and behavior. During these times, the funds did not trickle down through bank loans. It was practically impossible to take out a loan to purchase a house or start a business. No, the money went to reward executives with lavish vacations, parties, and other luxurious material matters. All while many families lost their homes, forced into foreclosure. In fact, the courts became a foreclosure mill for the banks. Yet, much of the bailout money was intended to be used for assisting families in distress with the possibility of avoiding foreclosure.

Meanwhile, the government saw jobs exported to other nations while millions of Americans were losing their jobs at home. Yet, the government did nothing to stem the tide. Who were they serving --the people or Corporate America? Is this the beginning of the dismantling of the United States of America -- a country founded on the basic principles of "a government by the people, for the people?"

Many people have been conditioned to believe that they are superior to other people by way of their social status, race, education, nationality, religion, sex, and just about every other reason one can think of. The list is endless! These are all illusions! Some people think that just because they are endowed with a lot of money that they also have a lot of power. But if you take away their money, they are really powerless. In fact, the bigger they are, the harder they fall.

The lust for power and control is one of many roots of all evil and sins which I will discuss throughout this book. This is certainly the case of the oligarchy's ambitions to dominate the world through a one world order ruled by private rich bankers who are oblivious to any law -- domestic and international – driven by a thirst for money and greed.[xii] No, the world needs to become one, but not in the direction of the oligarchy. The world belongs to mankind – not to a simple few people who feel entitled to all the powers of the world whose ultimate goal is to rule by dictatorship, not by democracy. These people are already in the process of dismantling the governments of the world. In the United States, there are daily attacks on the basic freedoms guaranteed by the Constitution and the Bill of Rights. A lot of companies in Corporate America do not respect the freedom of speech and expression in their organizations and go out of their way to silence those who attempt to reveal the truth -- especially against those who we know as "whistle blowers."

If you really want to trace the origins of all of man's problems, you can trace it all the way back to the beginning of mankind. As civilizations multiplied, so did different forms of societies and governments. When people started to migrate from their origins outwardly to the rest of the world, they created "boarders" among themselves. Some cases, natural barriers created separations between nations such as rivers, tributaries, mountain ranges and oceans. But as more nations came into existence, these "borders" became an illusional "dividing line" -- such as, between Canada and the United States. In one particular town, a simple street divides the two countries. On one side of the street, you would be in Canada. After passing through the border checkpoint, you would enter the US side of the same street.

One couldn't just merely cross the street in the middle of the block like in other cities.

Man has found ways to use money for the enslavement of other countries. People in these countries have to work tirelessly for very little while other more wealthy nations reap their harvests. Some nations are literally raped of their resources while the redistribution of these resources is limited and restricted by distributing entities more interested in maximizing their profits for a few, rather than benefitting mankind.

In a way, this has also led to limiting or restricting travel for many people. It would benefit the entire world if they could travel freely and learn about other cultures, races, and nationalities. It would be a wonderful and highly beneficial educational experience. However, man has limited this learning experience just for a small portion of the populace. He has, rather, opted to control education by limiting what people learn, how they learn, and in some cases, a many are not educated at all. Each human has a magnificent mind to learn, explore, and the potential to become highly educated, but more importantly, that everyone has the same educational opportunities. This is essential towards moving mankind in the right direction. Each human individual should be developed to his/her highest potential. The human mind was designed to explore the world, not just its immediate domain. Mankind was never meant to be separated neither from each other nor from God.

The problem is essentially simple – we have too many governments, too many nations, too many levels of inequitable currencies. I am not advocating a one world government ruled by an order whose agenda is merely to dictate to the world its own pleasures, enslave the people of the world while creating a police state, government-controlled media and entertainment, censorship, or a world order controlled by a group of people not elected by the people. People should be concerned when government officials want to move government services into private sectors – profit making entities. These companies are not out for the best interest of the people, but are only interested in making a profit at the expense of people. What is more worrisome in current times is that more paramilitary (mercenary) organizations are being used by the government to fight wars. This is only an indication that wars, too, have now become a profit-making activity. The danger signal is when governments begin to turn their countries into "police state" by outsourcing law enforcement agencies and prisons to private companies who are not accountable to government and laws enacted by the people, but enforce policies and mandates by corporations and special interests entities instead. Thus, denying the citizens of their basic freedoms of speech and expression and other rights bestowed to them by a constitution which would be totally invalidated if not recognized by its own government or law enforcement agencies. It just becomes merely meaningless "thoughts" on a piece of paper once treasured by the citizens of a country. For example, look at the City of Detroit. After it had declared bankruptcy, leadership of the city was handed over to the control of an appointed manager rather than a mayor elected by its citizens. The democratic process was denied the citizens of Detroit.

I advocate a democratic world government by the people and for the people whose focus is serving and benefitting the people of the world – a dynamic and living government willing to make adjustments and changes in order to serve people continually without having to rely on a form of what we knew as "currency"-- yet, one that is established on the principles of peace, democracy, rights, equality, and freedoms of speech, expression, religion, and press.

How can we do this, yet still guarantee equity of voice in government? Simply eliminate monetary systems and the inequitable distribution of money in the world. Presently, one can see the influence money has in politics and government when certain people wield a lot of money in the halls of government, much of which the average citizen does not have. Governments have been easily influenced by bribes, their law-making abilities have been highly tainted and influenced by special interests – especially when it comes time to vote on a bill or to sponsor legislation. Some people are given special preferential treatment and favors. Some are charged with unethical practices while others get away with more serious crimes. Yet, with all of this going on, the man with the small voice and bigger concerns, is constantly being drowned out.

Where the public wants this, the government does "that." Such as, where the people want peace, the government declares war – total polarity between the people and government -- as if to say the elected officials have put themselves on pedestals and have muted the voices of the people. Then, many people in government consider those in the minority as "the people." They typically voice the concerns of a relatively few number of people as representing the "majority" of the people – not even having their facts in order or correct.

As they say, "the rich get richer, the poor get poorer." And the divide between the two continues to increase. Leaders in government say that these people can find other jobs. Sadly, there are no more jobs to be had. One sign of an ineffective government is where leaders are not living in reality.

Also another product of the evilness of money is the rise of scam artists who have made their products or services look legitimate. Many are "pyramid schemes" designed to make people think they will make a lot of money, when -- in actuality -- they stand to lose a lot while the person at the top takes in all of their profits. Countless advertisements both in print and on the Internet appear daily enticing people to become members of their team. A lot of them will ask for huge investments to start, promising large sums of weekly or monthly money that will never come. Yet, they continuously ask for more money in the process.

In order for mankind to move in the right direction, he must find ways to eliminate the root sources of greed and corruption. This lesson was first taught when Sodom and Gomorrah was destroyed. It was again illustrated when Jesus had the encounter with moneychangers in the temple. The problem exists even today, but to a much greater degree. Man can and must find ways to live without the need or use for money. The practices associated with money have continued to separate man. One example is maintaining credit histories on people. These records have determined who can get financial credit, and who can't, all because of their credit scores. Those with bad credit scores are often denied employment, much of it not of their fault, but by unfortunate circumstances caused by other events. Yet, it was the individual that was blamed for these unfavorable events – such as being laid off, and unable to find suitable employment again. Yet these automated computer records only reflected that "they were delinquent" on paying their bills. Credit companies claim that these records are retained for a certain number of years – this is incorrect information. This mark followed them for the rest of their lives -- nor was it ever forgiven. Leaders of government never bothered to enact legislation to mandate expiration dates on these occasions to benefit the people/customers, but it wrote laws to benefit companies instead -- signs of an "unforgiving society."

The age of thinking and behaving that we are separate must soon come to an end – if we are to move in the right direction. Our behavior of separation has caused distrust, violence and wars between people not only between nations, but also within our own countries, cities and states.

The belief that we are separate have caused us to view and treat humans as being different just because of their color, race, nationality, religion, sex, and sexual orientation. Even within some religious groups, the male is considered more superior females. Many women are treated so poorly, they are often treated harshly with abuse, violence, and torture. Homosexuals are often viewed as anything but human beings. In some societies, they are even put to death including those whom have knowledge of their existence. In other cultures, they say they are granted equal rights and opportunities, but are really not treated equally – especially when religion has a strong influence in the matter – such as on the issue of marriage.

To move forward in the right direction we must shed our old beliefs, treat and respect each individual as human beings equally without regards to sexual orientation, color, race, creed, religion, nationality, or any other label we have a tendency of putting on people. We must shed the practice of putting labels on people – *period*.

The purpose of man's separation teaching was to simply break the spirit of mankind. That is, if he can successfully convince his fellow men that he is separated from God, then he can break their spirit and control behavior. In the next section, I am going to explain how man can regain his spirit by better understanding not only the Holy Trinity – but the inner trinity in him/herself.

SECTION THREE

UNDERSTANDING THYSELF

CHAPTER 8
THE BODY'S ONE FOUNDATION

Humans are a unique species of living beings on Earth. Our thinking, perspectives, and behavior caused some of us to believe that we were either created by a supreme creator, or evolved from other life forms. Many still demand factual evidence, some rely their assumptions based on mere theory. I am not particularly interested in the controversies of how humans were created either by creation or evolution. Who knows, it may as well have been a combination of both! The mere fact of humans is that we are all highly intelligent beings capable of creating, decision making, collaborating, making choices, inventing, and doing a wide variety of other things that other life forms cannot do.

Personally, I believe that God has created man evolving us, molding us from another existing life forms and instilling that unique quality in this particular animal we call "humans" – intelligence. After all, all humans have primitive animalistic characteristics despite having a high degree of intelligence. We all have the capabilities of hatred, fighting, violence, discrimination, and yes, even killing. But unlike other animal life forms, we have the ability of controlling these behaviors. We have the ability to make choices, the ability to discern the difference between good and bad, right and wrong. Man has the power to make wholesale changes to the world if he desires to do so – especially when the world he sees is not going in the direction that it should be.

In order for mankind to move in the right direction, each individual must first understand him/herself as a "whole individual." What do you mean "a whole individual?" As many of us only know and understand parts of ourselves. We work mainly with some parts of being, but we really have not learned how to function with all of ourselves as a "whole person." This is because in schools, churches, and homes, you were always taught that we were separate from these elements. Society has purposely guided you to think of these elements as separate and behave in such a manner in order to gain full control over the lives of many. It is how a relatively few number of the world's population are able to maintain their dominance and control in the world.

The first triad of a human pertains to the spiritual trinity in each of us. Some refer to it as the holy trinity – God, the Father, the Son, the Holy Ghost (Spirit). This lays the foundation in all of us – believers and non-believers alike. This concept can be found in many Christian denominations. It is, however, not found in all religions and has often been replaced by other worldly interpretations (like the trinity of the body which I will explain later on). All of this, however, was offered to cause chaos and confusion to the entire world. Different interpretations and understanding of this were created in order to separate man from God and to make him believe that he had always been separated from God, the Creator, the Son, and the Holy Spirit. The truth of the matter is, these are what make up the eternal pillars of each human being. This trinity is unique to humans and provides the "Living Light" not found in other living species. In the famous contemporary science fiction movie, *Star Wars*, there is the great phrase, "May the force be with you." In humans, *this is the force.*

God (The Creator, Our Father, Our Mother, The Great I Am) resides in each every individual. He is *always* with us – day in, day out. We are His creation as with everything else in this universe. The Bible says that we have been created in His image. This has always been disputed by creationists and evolutionists. Nevertheless, most lessons teach that God has always been a separate "higher being." God *is* *everything* and can take the form and shape of *anything.* He can appear and speak through us in animate or inanimate forms – through other life forms or non-life forms. Yes, even appearing through other people. The greatest example is when he appeared in the form of man through Christ Jesus. He can also use other people to speak for Him such as Abraham, Mohammed and Buddha, to name a few. Throughout history, many have served as His teacher both in ancient and contemporary times. Yet, often His word is often convoluted with interpretations of man or totally ignored.

The second factor in this triad is the Son. Christianity claims this to be Jesus Christ. This is where I depart from traditional theological beliefs. God may have sent many "sons" to Earth. Or, the same Son may have come to Earth many times in the form of different masters (teachers). Many people claim that there is only one way to Heaven – by believing only in Jesus Christ. Others claim that there are more than one way leading to Heaven.

Some describe Heaven as being a place with eight spokes. This is very similar to a symbol in Buddhism. Are Buddhists really talking about the same place when they talk about a destination called "Nirvana" or the "Pure Land?" John 14:6 says: "I am the Way, the Truth, and the Life. No one comes to the Father, but by Me." This would give Christians reason to believe that their way is the only way to Heaven. However, if The Son came to Earth many times before and after, and the Son resides in each of us, then there very well can be multiple paths to Heaven. John 14:2 says, "In my Father's house there are many dwelling places."

That is, if one believes that God and the Son are one of the same no matter if he [or she] be one of the same. It is not my objective to separate man and God, but to bring God and mankind together as one as He has originally envisioned.

Man has always assumed that God should always be on a pedestal – in a special place to be worshipped. The Bible illustrates this well. In ancient times, tribes made special tents to worship God. In modern times, people build magnificent temples, cathedrals, and buildings to honor Him. Elaborate ceremonies are held to worship Him. Many special prayers have been written especially dedicated for Him. He demands none of this. All he wants is closer, regular communion and fellowship with mankind in the form of plain ordinary conversation.

In Sunday meetings for worship, Quakers often have moments of silence to wait upon the Spirit as their form of communion. When He is within each of us, we really don't have to wait – just talk to Him directly.

But how is this done? Think of your body as the "House of the Lord." There is a physical "firewall." You have your inner "Internet cable" by means of your soul which establishes communication channels to the universe. The Holy Spirit is God's communication's channel to communicate with you. Connecting your line and God's line is a "modem" or a "router." Some might call it a WiFi channel. This is in the form of The Son depending on your spiritual beliefs. Some operate on "wireless" connections -- others have a "direct link." Internally, some work on different operating systems than others. Some are attracted to opposite operating system, others are attracted to like operating systems. We have no control over which operating system we are born with. We may have a totally different system than our parents. This cannot be changed either by our parents nor reprogrammed by schools or churches. It has been engrained in us like the read-only memory basic input/output system (ROM BIOS) on your computer system – it is genetically programmed. You can't see it, nor can you access it to change the program. It is "*hidden* and *read-only.*" In short, it doesn't matter which form of operating system you have or how you are connected, God communicates to all. He loves and cares for *all* humans. Many parents are notorious for disowning their children if they do not meet their expectations. In many countries, children are put out into the streets to survive for themselves. Some religious factions not only discriminate against people with different operating systems who are not compatible with theirs, but often, people they deem to be incompatible are put to death. Even having knowledge of incompatible people are given death sentences. God through His Son, in the form of all the masters of the World (Jesus Christ for example) have commanded us to love one another as God loves us all – unconditionally. Each individual has been specially pre-programmed with a special purpose – a unique destiny and mission on Earth. Allow each individual to explore and discover his or her destiny freely. This is why each individual has cognitive preferences. Do not force your preference on your child. *Offer* guidance, love and nurturing with a loving home to facilitate this growth and exploration.

Hence, educational institutions and systems must provide the mechanism for individual discovery and exploration freely.

This trinity represents the core in each of us.

CHAPTER 9
THE INNER TRINITY – THE THREE PILLARS

The building blocks of a human being begin at conception in the womb and continue to grow at birth. Although we do not recognize it as such, we each have a personal, inner trinity that constitutes our own unique framework – a structure beginning with childhood.

In childhood, we begin to explore new things in life. It is here when we take our first steps in life, start the long road on an educational path prescribed by local educational systems, exposed (or not) to religion or family beliefs and values, learn how to play by oneself, then with others, and so on. It is also during childhood that we learn certain behavioral patterns of being protective of one's possession, trust or distrust, like or dislike, right or wrong, good or bad. Some of us become more social while others become more introverted. It is during these early years where we develop our individual cognitive preferences that we carry throughout our schooling and adult years. It is at this period we develop our child-self in each of us -- our first pillar.

Then all of a sudden, we are thrown into a communal

system, like school, where our cognitive styles are stripped from us and we are expected to learn things according to "a standard." We may or may not adapt to these prescribed "standards." But, it's just society's way of developing people like "robots." Sometimes, these institutions are unaccommodating to special needs. Then, there are some systems which will provide special education only for those really in dire need for a special educational process while many others are "forced" into a process against their will.

A child's progress was really meant to be developed and evaluated most effectively as an individual – not on a "mass production" basis. Matthew 7:1 in the King James Bible says it best: "Judge not that ye not be judged." Too often, students are evaluated on a grading system comparing them against other students, then given a letter grade rather than evaluating each individual student on his or her own merits and accomplishments. This process of comparing one against another continues even though adulthood such as in employment and other competitive events.

While the child-self desires to continually learn, create, and explore; society, government and educational systems have developed ways to close the door on each individual very rapidly. The child-self in each of us never dies. It is always calling out to us wanting to come out and play. It represents the playful side in each individual no matter how young or old we are – even if a person is an elderly person, the child-self still resides. If we allow it, it can be our individual "guiding angel." However, as we grow into adults, we often become so busy with other adult activities that we very little give the child-self fewer opportunities to play – for example, going to the ocean, mountains, lakes, forests, amusement parks, or just a local municipal park in general. Remember what

I said about taking care of the body. This is the child's way of saying, "Take care of *me*."

The second pillar of our framework is the adult-self. It is essentially a continuation of the child-self only at an adult level with adult activities, such as working either for an employer or self-employment. But it also involves decision making, financial matters (personal and business), political issues, adult relationships, and other activities and events that were not experienced at the childhood level. In short, there are much more responsibilities and expectations. Typically, adults are more accountable for their behavior and actions.

The skills that we learned as children by learning how to create, invent, and apply special skills are carried through adulthood into the workplace. They can be very beneficial to companies. Employment is a form of "adult play." It's a place where the child-self can release these energies. However, in modern times, since most people tend to ignore the needs of the child-self let alone that this element still exist, they have eliminated the "adult playground" in many countries by way of exporting jobs overseas, laying off employees, and minimizing unemployment benefits. Because of this tragedy, many have lost their homes and are forced to live in the streets. Yet many people expect them to still behave in a civil manner while they have just treated them as "animals" and have made little or no further accommodations or provisions for their safety or well being. If society elects to remove the pillar of the adult-self from individuals, then these folks will return to an animal state – it's only their basic instinct of survival.

The parent-self in each individual serves in an authoritarian role which provides wisdom and guidance in each of us. This represents the third pillar in each of us. It provides us essential parenting skills when we nurture future generations through our children and the ability to pass along our values and beliefs as well. That's not to say that our children should be expected to accept our personal values and/or beliefs. Broken families often result because parents try to force their values and religious and/or personal beliefs on their children. Love your children for who they are – as unique, free individuals – not exact clones of yourselves. Give your children the room to grow and develop the way they choose. Yes, help and guide them on their path, for the journey will be short and narrow. But at one point, give children a "jumping off point," there will be a time of departure where they will follow their own way, not yours -- do not be disappointed, for it is their destiny.

The child-, adult-, and parent-selves create the three internal pillars or the framework of a human being. These elements are so transparent, many do not realize they are all part of us. Yet, they influence our daily lives subconsciously on one dimension. Why on one dimension? Many in the world are totally unaware that there is a third-dimension in our lives. Some totally ignore the third dimension, yet others give more credibility or preference to one over the other.

This dimension that I have just discussed pertains to the trinity of the body – like the framework of a building. These three pillars are what make human beings unique from other forms of life on Earth. However, when one pillar or more is taken away from an individual, it can be very detrimental to the character of that person. An individual can literally be reduced to a state of an animal. Unfortunately, man has discovered ways to do this. Some examples are through deprivation of life's needs and essentials (like homes and jobs), torture, isolation, discrimination, racism, social classes and many other ways.

The next triad creates the outer walls of the building.

CHAPTER 10
THE SPIRITUAL TRINITY

To start, we are all blessed with a unique *BODY*. At birth, we are born, usually intersexed or transgendered with either predominant male or female characteristics with unique *MINDS*. We all have a responsibility to ourselves as well as to the world to take care of our bodies, our "vessels," through proper nutrition, exercise and medical care.

External industrial forces have provided destructive mechanisms that are detrimental to our bodies. Many of these products cause obesity and other health issues that were in existence when man was first created. Governments are also of no help, for they endorse these efforts in order to promote profits for corporations and write legislation against efforts that would promote a healthier lifestyle and food products. Like, "it's okay if it will benefit the few at the expense of the masses." Yet, there is also very little regard for the wellbeing of Mother Earth herself.

The body is a "temple." Some say it is a "Temple of God." Others have a different perspective on this same idea. Yet, others don't even think that this is true. This is, perhaps, the reason why nations send people to wars – because they feel they are expendable. The *body is holy*. Each person has an element of divinity residing within him or herself regardless if it is a spiritual-divinity or a self-divinity. *Life is sacred and precious.*

The body must have the opportunity of communing with the natural elements of God. Natural life has a lot to offer – especially in forms of nurture through a balance of outdoor life (air and sunlight), water (ocean and rivers), mountains (trees and forests). The natural elements of Earth also provide other benefits and opportunities for the mind and soul as well which I will explain a little more in just a while.

The mind drives and controls every function of our body, sends essential electrical signals from the brain to the various parts of the body to cause motion and movement, and especially cause humans to do what other life forms cannot do – speak in the form of languages. All life forms can communicate, but humans have the ability to talk in intelligent forms. It is only in different forms of languages where people become frustrated when they cannot understand what other people are talking about, misinterpret what they are saying, then lead to a misunderstanding – sometimes to a level of distrust, anger and even violence.

The soul has often been an element of misunderstanding. It has always been assumed that the soul resides within each individual. This is totally incorrect. The soul envelops the whole person. The soul is so large that it spans the universe. The soul is the body and mind's connection to the universe. When the body dies, the soul continues to live. Sometimes, part of the soul departs the planet. When our body sleeps at night, our soul is awake and active. Or, it takes us into a dream state into a world of imagination. Occasionally, we experience visiting other civilizations in other galaxies. The soul never sleeps but constantly watches guard over us. It helps us to see things to come and helps our mind communicate messages without speaking a word. The soul is that which binds the mind and body.

So, the mind, body, and soul make complete the whole you – as a human. In the next chapter, I'll discuss how this all ties together. Because even though we very much act and behave as individuals, we are all connected to not only to each other, but to everything in this universe.

CHAPTER 11

THE INTERSECTING THE TRIANGLES FOR TOTAL SELF-BALANCE

In putting the pieces together, there are portions of a human being which make up the "total person." When these panels are joined together, they make a three-sided triangle. Coincidentally, we are reminded of this by physical structures on Earth -- such as the great pyramids of Egypt. The science of surveying uses a process of triangulation (using 3 points) to determine heights or depths often called "leveling."

Typically, it takes at least three points to establish a good, balanced foundation. We have this in the form of the spiritual trinity. Some use the form of the Father, the Son, and the Holy Spirit. Our structure, like that of a building, is comprised of our child-, adult-, and parent-selves. These are like the steel beams of a building. They are there, but we cannot see them. Finally, there are the walls created by the mind, body and spirit. We can see and hear these things by the words we speak and through our actions. To take away any of these elements diminishes the whole person. Some societies have successfully found ways to degrade the whole person though various forms of body (physical) and sensory controls.

Other people feel that some elements are unimportant in their lives and disregard them. For people like these, there are typically signs of unbalance in their lives, for they often encounter societal, behavioral, mental, emotional, and financial problems. Especially those people who try to live without the existence of the spiritual trinity. These are the people who try to do things on their own and often encounter failure in their lives, often at the expense and sacrifice of others.

For each person to move forward in the right direction, each individual must realize the importance of every element and component which makes him or herself as a human being. Disregard for any of these will result much like a crippled airliner taking off a runway – in a stall. Some may not take off. Others will take off, crash, and take many people with them. Every component of a human is important and must be respected and treated with equal care and without regard to prejudice or discrimination.

By recognizing these elements within us, we gain and understand our full capabilities and power given to us by the Creator. By understanding that within and around ourselves, we come to better understand that all are not separated, but connected.

The church is not a building, mosque, cathedral, or physical temple. We each are "A Temple of God." We can, in our own unique ways, elect to worship God in a corporate manner such as in physical venues, or in a private, secluded setting. But in reality, He is always present within us. Many of us have found ways to turn Him off – to shut Him out of our lives. He is not angered by this. The Creator's presence is a switch that had been built into us at birth. He continually cares about and for each of us. And so, He quietly resides in each individual whether you've turned Him on or out. Many people have tuned Him out and have become too busy doing other things on and by their own. Many people in governments and companies have become complacent to this as well. They have all disregarded their foundations – their spiritual trinity -- hence all the chaos and problems of the world.

In order to move in the right direction, the entire world must elevate its ability to think in multiple dimensions. While we all have this capability, practically all of us never use it. Living species on other galactic civilizations think, behave, and act on a higher level. Humans on Earth lag far behind. Not because they are incapable of doing so, but because people are stubborn, lazy, and are refuse to change their ways for a much better life. Leaders in government are especially notorious for thinking and legislating on one dimension – on one axis. In the United States, for example, this dilemma of working on one plane has caused polarity. Only two political parties serve in major governmental roles at the national, state and local levels. As I have mentioned previously, in order to attain complete balance, it takes three points to level a field. With only two political parties making major decisions and policies for a nation, the country is just spinning its wheels and not really moving in a direction – it is stuck and will continue to be stuck until it allows for at least a third major political party that is quite different from the two presently serving the country -- especially when the two major parties don't offer the nation real choices, but are easily swayed by profit making entities influencing their decisions with money.

We continually have a habit of thinking and making decisions according to the past and tradition. Society has always been afraid of letting go of the past and working towards the future. The early years of the twenty-first century have been no different than the latter years of the twentieth century. People have been slow to change, yet still live by their habitual tendencies of solving their problems through violence and wars. The United States, in particular, wastes a huge amount of dollars on national defense. For example, examine the federal income tax breakdown for each dollar United States citizens paid to the Federal Government in the following table:

For each dollar of federal income tax citizens paid in 2010, the United States

Government spent about:

39¢ - Pentagon spending for current and past wars	4¢ - Veterans
	6¢ - Interest on Pentagon Debt
	28¢ - Pentagon and Related Spending
20¢ - Health Care	
17¢ - Responding to Poverty	
14¢ - General Government	9¢ - Interest on Public Debt
	5¢ - Government Operations
6¢ - Supporting the Economy	
3¢ - Energy, Science and Environment	
2¢ - Diplomacy, Development and War Prevention	

"Where Did Our Income Tax Dollars Go?" Friends Committee on National Legislation, Washington, D.C. (October 2010) http://fcnl.org/assets/issues/budget/taxchart11.chart.pdf

As Matthew 6:21 says, "For where your treasure is, there will your heart be also."

Other industrial nations are probably not as far different in their spending habits from the United States. But in order to wean ourselves off our past behavior and practices and really begin to make changes in the world and in governments, mankind on Earth needs to expect and demand changes. If a government cannot adapt itself to new and improved ways of thinking outside the box, then it must be changed and replaced by the people. The people must not become complacent with a form of government just because it has been around for two-hundred years without any changes or modifications – especially if it has obviously continued on a downward spiral. As with automobiles, airliners, and human beings – these all require continuous periodic routine maintenance in order to ensure optimum performance. A government is no exception to this rule. Changes do not necessarily have to come by way of a violent revolution, military takeover, or civil war. But in order to ensure that the government remains honest and open for improvement is to establish and create unbiased citizen oversight agencies, not its own internal auditing departments.

Jesus Christ was the greatest teacher in history. During his time on Earth, He taught man to think outside of the box – in multiple dimensions – by sharing numerous parables. The lessons of these parables can still be applied in modern times. We need to constantly consider and apply alternative answers and solutions for the benefit of mankind even if they be contrary to traditional beliefs, practices and "standard procedure."

If we all valued our individual components as human beings, we would learn to respect and care for each other's understanding that we are all connected through God. Thinking at a higher level requires us to modify our belief system in multiple dimensions – not just a one or two-dimensional system as we have been accustomed to. We all need to move forward and learn to think at least three-dimensionally, if not more and on multiple layers. Every one of our brains has this unique capability. It is far superior than a typical hard drive or memory chips in a computer system.

Each human in the world must have the opportunity to excel and succeed in life as highly unique individuals. We all have been born equally with the same unique elements. Respect it as such so that individuals are provided with a fair and equitable opportunity to succeed. Change your educational systems and institutions for equality and fairness based on individual accomplishments, achievements, and potential – not a fabricated, faulty grading system.

Recognition, respect, and care for these elements in a human being ensure a balance in the world, in society, and among nations. Many of the problems the world faces today are because people, including leaders, are living unbalanced lives. At least one or more of these nine elements are missing from their lives. And what I have outlined in the previous chapters only establishes the framework of existence as a balanced human being. To fully understand the way of living as a balanced human being, I highly recommend reading *The Middle Theory – A Guide to Balance* by Deshon M. Fox.[xiii] Mr. Fox does a wonderful job explaining the importance of maintaining balance in one's personal life as it also relates to relationships, family, God, and the power to move mountains. His book should be read by everyone for he offers great solutions to solving the problems of the world through his "Middle Theory." The planet truly is "out of balance" and needs to find it once again.

Like walking on a long narrow path, moving in the right direction requires total balance. Being out of balance on this journey will cause you to fall over the edge on one side or the other. It would be like walking a tight rope. This journey will require absolute focus and perseverance in order to reach the final goal.

CHAPTER 12
INTERCONNECTIONS OF SELF

One of the major themes of this book is that we, as individual human beings, are not alone. We *are* connected not only to each other but to every life form on this planet. We are connected to everything in this universe by God via our individual souls. There is an excellent song entitled *We Are All Connected* by Symphony of Science which describes us as being connected to everything – ourselves, the earth, and the universe. Part of the lyrics describe how:

> *"We are all connected;*
> *To each other, biologically,*
> *To the earth, chemically,*
> *To the rest of the universe, anatomically."*[xiv]

This is very true, particularly from a scientific point of view. The song also continues to describe the fact that we *are* but "microscopic specks" in this universe – like the stars, only smaller. Biologically, we are related to each other through physical traits and characteristics, anatomically, and a complex DNA structure which gives us our very own unique individual qualities.

As with our connectivity to the Earth, we possess and are made up of similar earthly elements used for other purposes. Unfortunately, some of those elements have been genetically engineered by man and have found their way into daily human consumption that are not compatible with the human body and often pose destructive forces our lives -- man has found ways to "legally" poison himself through modern industrial technology and manufacturing processes. Instead of finding ways to live naturally and in co-existence with Earth and the environment, he continues to find ways to distance himself by separating himself from the laws of the Creator by placing himself on a pedestal and continuing to think that he is a more superior being than other living creatures. Since man is connected with the Earth, he must return to finding ways of living in harmony with it, rather than in discord. By living in discord, man has certainly made other life forms extinct either through pollution, poisoning, over-harvesting, and just about every other mismanagement practice that mankind has carried out all because he was given dominion over the Earth. Moreover, this was all done in the name of profit.

Anatomically, we are connected to this universe. Our atoms and molecules are made up of similar substances found in space as well as from this Earth. However, the alignment of these atoms and molecules are what make us unique as human beings.

There is one element that the song does not include. Although we are connected to everything on this Earth through our biology, chemistry, and anatomical features, there is one major ingredient that uniquely connects all humans together which is not a scientific component. That is, we are connected spiritually whether you believe this or not. There is a divine, driving Light within each individual which inspires and provides our unique gift for intelligence, reasoning, and problem solving that makes us unique from other life forms. It is an "internal four-way switch" within all of us. It is like driving a car. When you want to drive forward, place the gear in "drive;" to make the car go backwards, you move the gear in "reverse;" and to let the car stay in place, place the gear in either "neutral" or "park."

Where it is said that art imitates life, it also can be said that technology mimics people – or vice versa. People very much act like cars. People who have this divine light turned on are in "drive," they appear to be in a forward motion, motivate people to move forward, and are typically inspirational and motivational types. These enlightened folks are concerned about the care and wellbeing of all humanity, possess high levels of wisdom, spirituality, and common sense and live in truth -- not only true to themselves, but are true to others. They may be identified as great leaders, yet there are also people less known who possess the equal and same qualities. There are several levels of these people like in an automobile with a manual transmission. Those in "high gear" or appear to be "cruising" are very few. There are a few more in "second gear" and many are just starting out in "first gear" – those who are just beginning to discover themselves.

Many are either in "neutral" or "park." That is, they have made little progress either forward or backward. And then, there are those who refuse to move at all – these are the ones who are just stagnant in life, refusing to accept change. Then, unfortunately for the world, there are many who think they are going forward, but their gear is actually in "reverse." Sadly, many leaders of countries are in this mode. They give people the illusion that they are taking their countries in the "right direction." In actuality, they've plotted reverse course. The divine guiding light has been extinguished and they are, instead, self-motivated only using rhetoric to mask over their true agenda. The indicators are their behavior. They may say and promise one thing, but in reality, they will reverse their promises and take action contrary to what they have said. Some people refer this using a term called "false truths." Others use a more direct term called "lying." Unfortunately, the people who are in reverse often stall-out those who are in forward motion through deceit, misbehavior, covert and despicable practices. Some are carried out as if they were normal and legitimate. These people often try to silence those who are in forward motion by denying the most basic human freedoms of speech and expression. If they are not successful at doing this, then these individuals are often denied the ability to travel freely or are incarcerated.

People in reverse do whatever it takes to prevent change and progress. These are the people satisfied with the status quo. They are often closed minded and will often debate and fight any suggestion of change. If they are forced into making changes, they will often stall or procrastinate. If people want to go one way, they will attempt to move in another.

Throughout history, man has always tried to distance himself from God, always believing that man and God are separate. For example in Genesis 3, the book of beginnings, mankind, through Adam and Eve were exiled out of the Garden of Eden by God because of sin for they had eaten from the tree of knowledge. Therefore, their exile was their punishment for the act of sinning. It is said that sin causes separation from God. Another example where man was separated from God can be found in Genesis 11 where people of a holy line were scattered all over the face of the earth. After Babel, the scattered people were not only separated from that holy line, but also from God's word which Shem's family preserved and passed down from Adam, Seth, Enoch, Noah, Shem, and Abraham.

God has, throughout history, always tried to communicate to mankind through other men such as the great founders of the world's religions. However, by distancing himself, man has always attempted to silence God by "silencing the messenger." And the "messenger" can be in the form of practically anything – not just a person such as in the form of Jesus who was crucified on the cross. God can communicate to us through trees, rocks, water, and practically everything else. Take trees for example, man has done a disservice to the future of humility by destroying rain forests and clearing natural wilderness areas in the name of "progress and development." Since the beginning of humanity, man has attempted to replace God's world with his (man's). The natural foods that God had provided for mankind have been replaced by processed staples. This has led to dire and deadly consequences including diseases only known in the modern age. Yet, legislation is passed to prohibit the growth of natural, sustainable foods, only protecting those which result in a profit for special interests – not for the benefit of mankind (i.e., genetically modified organisms [GMOs]).

American Bison (buffalo) is another example of a life form that faced near extinction. Native Americans used the entire animal after it was killed. The whole carcass was used for food, clothing and shelter. However, when settlers moved west, they only slaughtered the animal only for their hide and, perhaps a few other parts. The rest of it was left to rot on the prairie – it's meat from the carcass spoiled and was unfit for consumption by Native Americans.

Man has developed the habit of being very wasteful. He often rapes Mother Earth of her resources, but hasn't taken necessary steps to replenish them. Some nations are good at maximizing their available resources, others are notoriously and excessively wasteful. Some countries go to war in order to gain access over another country's assets, they pillage everything the nation has leaving it barren with nothing left for the people. In the process of doing so, the "victorious nation" attempts to instill its values and beliefs on the loser – much of it is compatible and does not settle well with the citizens. As a result, there is additional hostility. Many countries in Africa have been victims of this phenomenon. Often embattled through wars, they have been pillaged and left barren. Many of their inhabitants have been left with brutal dictators resulting in a land of starving people with very little international aid. Unfortunately, in many cases the nations would be left barren, scarred, defaced, and uninhabitable forever.

When man set himself in reverse, he created separate values and beliefs that were different from God's. It was a total departure from the Golden Rule, which was shared and compatible among all civilizations. When man added his own twist to this rule, this is where differences settled between nations and religions. Rather than tearing walls down that separate himself from his fellow man, he has continuously strived to build higher walls and bigger borders. An example of this is the wall being built along the border between the United States and Mexico. Another example is that dividing Israel and Palestine. The lesson to be learned is that *all* walls were meant to be torn down -- especially if they were built to divide and separate people. The classic example of this was the wall that divided East and West Berlin.

Whereas we are connected with God, so are people

connected to each other through God regardless of their national domicile. If you truly seek immigration reform, build bridges and railways, and find ways to bring yourselves closer – not separate yourselves further by building walls. In fact, this not only applies to the region between the United States and Mexico, but to the entire world. Shed your borders for Earth is the dominion of mankind – not by governments or secret societies. This is a world that was designed to be managed by the people and for all living beings – not by one particular group, race, special interest or handful of people.

Whatever is done for the rich, must be done for the poor and everybody in between the spectrum. Whatever is done for Christians, must also be done equally for Jews, Muslims, Buddhists, and all other faiths. Whatever care and concern is done for mankind must also be done for Mother Earth and all of her species.

SECTION FOUR

VISION FOR HUMANITY

OPENING REMARKS TO SECTION FOUR

Countless other articles, books and papers have offered visions of humanity in the past – some by groups of people, some by individuals. What I have to offer is only a vision from my own perspective as a visitor – a traveler in this universe. Hopefully, this offers the start of a grander vision for humanity.

Many ideas offer an excellent direction of how mankind should move. But when you take a look all of them, they go off in many separate directions as I have said earlier. This will be harmful in leading mankind in one direction for productive change so that a major transformation can actually occur in the history of mankind. Humanity cannot move in a common direction if the world's population remains splintered with different ideals, beliefs, values, and closed minds. Nor can these changes occur if world leaders force them on the people of the world by brute force, particularly when there has been no input or "buy-in." They will be totally rejected.

For changes to occur, the process has to be an interactive, participatory course that not only demands feedback from those who have been identified as "highly gifted, educated, and influential," but also from those, lesser known as well. In short, the process of developing the grandest vision for humanity requires the participation of the broadest spectrum of the world's populace. But more importantly, it demands absolute openness, without prejudice or personal preferences. The focus must be on the total benefit to mankind without regard to race, gender, sexual orientation, color, religion, or nationality.

A comprehensive vision for humanity will affect all walks of life. In order to create the grandest vision, input from all of life's aspects are needed. In the next few chapters, I will touch upon some of the aspects of life which I feel need further growth and adjustment in order to create that "better world" for humanity.

CHAPTER 13
GOVERNMENT AND POLITICS

Thus far, my focus has been mainly on the government of the United States. In this chapter I am going to focus my concentration on global scale. Governments can either be effective in facilitating moving mankind in the right direction, or, they can be a detrimental barrier inhibiting progress. A classic example of this is when the Israelites broke their bondage from slavery out of the hands of Pharaoh in Egypt in ancient times only to be thrown obstacles in their path to freedom -- such as the chariots pursuit of the Israelites to the sea just before Abraham parted the waters. Another example of this is when the King of England sent his armies to the New World to end the revolutionary cause of the American colonists' fight for independence. There is a lesson to be learned – *the will of the people will always be triumphant over its government.*

Another contemporary example is where the people in Berlin triumphed over Communist rule and tore down a wall that separated their nation, thus uniting East and West Germany.

Unfortunately, like the cells in our bodies, nations find ways of splitting and becoming separate nations. Most recently, there has been the creation of North and South Sudan – more borders leading to separation of people.

One of the major elements that divide countries is the matter of currencies. This, I will discuss in a subsequent chapter. For now, I will focus on other matters pertaining to government and politics. As with life itself, government and politics must be balanced. Of course, there will be times of disagreement as to how to proceed on matters. But, God has given humans a unique ability to reason – to solve problems logically and diplomatically without the need for violence and war. Throughout time, people have created superficial barriers between themselves that have created mistrust, animosity, disunity, favoritism, prejudice, racism, hatred, egotistical pride, and just about everything else to cosmetically make oneself "look better than the other." The focus of attention has turned to "me" rather than "us." "What's good for our nation…" rather than "What's good for the world…" People have put themselves on pedestals and act as if they were a "deified god" worthy to be worshipped while everyone else is, to say the least, *worthless*. Governments, rather than managing the behavior of its people, have let bad behavior run rampant and out of control. Political leaders are easily manipulated and corrupted. Just about every entity on this Earth teaches and promotes the idea of separation – in schools, churches and in government. In a way, these are ideals that have always been passed down through generations. These habits have been instilled in man for a very long time. But now, it is time to break bad habits.

Many will look to their governments for moving mankind forward. In order for the governmental component to help in this matter, all governments of the world will have to shed their old ways of doing business and unite towards one common goal of moving mankind in the right direction. Not for their own self-national pride or preferences, but for the sake of humanity – moving forward as one race – a human race, regardless of nationality, color, ethnicity, or sexual orientation.

What is that goal? Coming together as one world -- a singular nation -- one free of borders, where citizens can travel without the need for a passport -- a democracy truly by the people and for the people of the world. There will, perhaps be regional governments to manage designated areas or zones, but these areas will not be created to keep people out nor serve one group of people.

Hence, political leaders will need to be more servant-like to the people rather than being bought off by major profit-making entities. Bribery will no longer be tolerated in the halls of legislation. Old laws and policies will be abandoned and new ones created to reflect modern, changing times. Laws, rather than remaining static, would become living resources of policy to reflect on ever changing times rather than forcing generations to live by old and outdated standards of living. Laws which "clutter" halls of government will be removed from the books – especially if they are no longer applicable to current times. And, laws that do not reflect the needs of the world, will also be eliminated. Government in every form will be streamlined to maximize efficiency and become more cost effective.

One major way of doing this, particularly when the world moves to a singular world government, is the elimination of national armies – especially for offensive purposes. Militaries would play an entirely different role in peaceful missions such as during of emergencies such as national disasters. And since the world would become one nation, there would be no need to declare war against each other. War would become a thing of the past.

To begin moving in the right direction, nations must begin to shed all of the barriers which separate themselves. Not only by removing their borders, but also by disarming itself. Some nations have more than enough nuclear weapons to destroy the entire planet. Others have absolutely none. This madness must cease immediately. Governments can play a major role in stopping these trends by not funding resources to manufacture such products, nor by exporting such products to other countries. Large and powerful countries must take the lead in disarmament by resisting the temptation to build more weapons and take initiatives to effectively reduce their armament to nothing – zero.

If you are going to gain the respect from another species (i.e., human to another animal) – try removing all of your clothing and do it in your birthday suit! To other animals, your clothing presents a barrier and an aura of suspicion. It masks your soul creating a sense of mistrust for that particular animal – especially if it is not familiar with you like your dog or cat -- this way, you are not hiding anything. The same principle applies when you are trying to gain the respect of your fellow citizens of the Earth – shed all your weapons and armaments and wear only what is necessary to keep you covered up. But, this also includes that which is in your mind as well – communicate in a clear mind. Do not communicate for peace with a hidden agenda. *Peace must come unconditionally with no strings attached.*

The coming together as one world must include nations and continents which are often left out of worldly discussions. These include the countries in Africa and Latin (Central and South) Americas. All too often, major discussions directing the world have been among the richest nations of the world and often left out the impoverished nations. Each nation must have an equal voice. We must all have a common understanding of each other. This includes building better relations such as finding permanent peace between Israel and neighboring Arab countries. And to elevate this, finding peace and building better relations between Arab countries and the Western World.

The United States has been insistent on spreading its form of democracy to nations of the world. I believe this to be wrong. I am in favor of a democratic world. But not by a "democracy" that is tainted and influenced by corporate corruption and special interests. This is not my ideal democracy. The ideal democracy is what the Founding Fathers of the United States constructed in the original Constitution and framework of the country -- a government by the people and for the people. Not a government bought off and influenced by corporate money and advertising where leaders are bribed by special interests groups. A government that is totally free from external influences, control, and strings attached.

Many nations take the proverbial "cowboy" attitude, "an eye for an eye, a tooth for a tooth." They would much rather shoot first, ask questions later. This often leads countries into more troubles than they can handle. Do not be afraid of opening up lines of communications. In ancient days, leaders used to confront other leaders directly. The problem is in contemporary times, leaders are not bold enough to do these themselves – they frequently send emissaries to do their negotiations. National leaders need to lead their nations, not just sit behind desks and talk before television cameras and microphones. *Be bold and act boldly.* For the first time since 1979, an American President, Barak Obama, communicated by way of a telephone conversation with the President of Iran,

Hassan Rouhani. This has broken a thick wall of ice which separated two mistrusting countries and opened the doors for further communications and diplomacy.[xv]

CHAPTER 14
ECONOMY/WORLD CURRENCIES

The phrase, "money is the root of *all* evil..." is true. Or more accurately, money can be viewed as a "tool" for such evil. *Greed* is actually the root of this evil. Money has been used to limit resources and human services, it has been hoarded, worshipped, caused economic and personal hardships, and people have even lost their lives over money and financial issues. Nations and municipalities have gone bankrupt because of the lack of money. Governments bailout corporations with taxpayers' money, but they do very little to aid their fellow citizens. Mankind cannot move forward in the right direction as long as it is dependent on a form of currency of any kind. Some nations are more well-off than others. Many nations are very poor. Some nations are so poor that they are often slaves to other wealthier countries -- scandalized and raped for their resources. People in these countries suffer poverty, starvation, malnutrition, poor living conditions, struggle through internal strife, chaos, civil war, and ruthless dictators.

The world must wean itself of the dependency on

money and learn how to live in a currency-free society. Some organizations, such as the Venus Project, suggest a Resourced-based Economy[xvi] which suggests a currency/money-free system. In my book, *Kami Jin,* I offered the thought of creating a universal life credit system where everyone is guaranteed 25-million life credits per year (one credit equaling either one dollar or one Euro). Whatever the concept or system, it would certainly simplify the current complicated structure of different national currencies managed by a World Bank that controls different interest rates, values and devalues currencies of countries, plummets nations into financial turmoil, etc. Furthermore, the current currencies of the world displace people into poverty, homelessness, and cause starvation in poor countries. For mankind to move forward in the right direction, humanity must move all peoples onto the same level playing field -- this means, no one nation is superior or inferior to the other. All nations are equally the same with identically high standard of living. Stronger nations will have to come to the aid of weaker nations without regard to costs. For when the currencies of the world are eliminated, the issue of costs will not be a burden. Unfortunately, weaning oneself off of a currency system will not occur overnight. It will, perhaps, take generations to become reality. But the process of doing so must begin right away. Of course, there will be major resistance for changes will be hard to come by. But this is all in the process of transitioning to a world of higher thinking and intelligence.

Sad to say, those who are not open to a currency-free world will not be able to move forward. Their personal values, focus and attention to money will weigh them down. It is imperative that humanity move lightly with very little to carry. For in the creation of a new world, there will be no use for an old currency system. In a new world, there will be no use for money at all. Even when you pass away, you cannot take your money with you. The concept is the same here in moving humanity in the right direction. Humanity will start afresh with a new set of values, old things will pass away – this includes an antiquated currency system.

The current monetary system was designed to serve only an exclusive few of the world's so called elite. The value of material things is only a man-made illusion that can be changed in a flash. The Buddha said that *everything* is impermanent. Hoarding money to become "rich" will get you nowhere in this world. Man has placed value on things which really have no value in this universe at all. Yet the things that do have precious worth, you place absolutely no value at all -- such as, the value of human life. Politicians send people to war to bid their fighting and lay down their precious lives for political causes and needs. Yet the politicians turn around and say that it's good for the people's freedom and safety. Yet, the politicians are not the ones that actually go to war and do the fighting.

The quality and standard of living is defined by man. These standards are different among various nations and are not the same. In some countries, the standards of living are higher than others. To define that high level of standard, nations must come together in agreement and shed barriers that prevent all nations from experiencing the same high quality standards of living throughout the entire world. To do this, nations must rid the world of an inequitable currency system were currencies in some countries are more valuable than others. The playing field must be leveled and equalized. To do this is to rid the world of a currency system as we know it, altogether. Currencies in a new world are an antiquated idea that would no longer serve a purpose in civilization in the future. With lifestyles flourishing throughout the world, the planet can longer endure something that limits resources and supplies to a growing world's population.

Look at the palaces that you dwell in, compared to the tin shacks and cardboard dwellings that can be found in shantytowns around the world – starving people scavenging for just one meal a day at best if that.

Live well, my friend, for all this will come to pass. In the new world, there will be no classes of people. Everyone will live in affluence regardless of your "supreme efforts" to maintain your illusion of superiority. Humanity will rise to the level of greatness as a free people not ruled by a corporate machine planning on the obsolescence of mankind. History only proves time and again, that man will not succumb to tyranny.

History also shows that many civilizations also manage to survive without money. The world needs to learn lessons from these ancient civilizations. All-in-all, the entire world has become very complex. It need not be so – especially when the world becomes one. People can live in an elegant, sophisticated, modern world, yet with a simplified government free of a currency system. Money is a bad habit that the world must learn how to break in order to survive. People have been conditioned to believe that money is conditional to our survival – it is not. Food, water, and energy are necessary for our survival. Mankind can easily remove the currency value of these commodities when it learns how to live without money. Where man has a habit of placing a monetary value on everything like the proverbial label gun, he can easily say that the same commodity has absolutely no value at all – the label can easily be removed.

When people learn how to remove these labels from everything, then crime will also be reduced. The lust for material things and possessions will no longer become a factor. It's as to say, "If you want something I have, take it. I can easily replace it without cost."

If a house burns down, the community would join in to rebuild a new one at no or very little cost. In a small part of the United States, they still do this even today such as in Pennsylvania Amish Country in Lancaster, Pennsylvania.

The dynamics of the workforce would also dramatically change. There would be no need for insurance and people would labor purely for the enjoyment of working for a common cause. Corporations would not pay their employees, but would have to find other incentives for people to work for their companies. More importantly, this would allow companies to devote their attention to research and development. Health care for all would then become a fundamental human right, not a privilege for only those who can afford it.

Lastly, governments and politicians of the world must take all necessary steps to eliminate the sales and distribution of weapons designed to destroy life. Since the beginning of mankind, man has suffered enough due to the ignorance and stubbornness of others who have refused to take the necessary steps to eliminate guns and ammunition from the streets of the world. The greed for money and material lust amplified the frequency of homicides throughout the modernization of mankind. Heaven sends its pleas for this madness to cease once and for all. In the new world, there will be no need for armaments. When money in the world is eliminated, there will be no need to kill or steal for money or one's possessions. Furthermore, besides eliminated the sales and distribution of weapons internally within nations, countries must also cease to sell abroad. All manufacturing of weapons and products designed to destroy man and what he has created must come to an end. Failure to do this will result in the ultimate destruction of mankind all because of his arrogance, stubbornness, and unwillingness to change from the "cowboy" mentality. Be still and heed the pleas, warnings and messages from Heaven. Listen well to your spiritual leaders who forewarn that you are being led in the wrong direction taking the masses with you.

The days of living in the "Wild West" are history. Man must learn his lessons and move on into the future. Life, by all means, must be preserved – both human life and all other life forms on this planet. Don't sink Mother Earth just for your sake! Lead as servants of the people – not for special interests who bribe and corrupt you with blood money.

CHAPTER 15
RELIGION

Like world governments, religions of the world can either be instrumental in leading mankind in the right direction, or they can serve as a major barrier. It is my prayer that religions will shed their differences and find common ground to lead inspire humanity onto the right course. Naturally, this will not be easy. As we have discovered at the beginning of this book, many religions have been formed since the beginning of mankind. Many of the disagreements, as evidenced in Chapter 1, have resulted in splinter groups and new religions. My belief is that when man was created, there was only one religion – the relationship between man and the Creator. There was only one basic, principle rule *[using the positive form]:* "One should treat others as one would like others to treat oneself."

Throughout history, however, things have become complicated. Men have added to this, as we have discovered. We know that each religious belief has its own version of the Golden Rule. But every religion is guilty of adding its own unique "twist" to life. Fascinating, however, that religious customs and traditions have led to a wide variety of different interesting cultures and life styles. Unfortunately, they have also led to conflicts and disagreements as to who lives in the "right way." Some are led to believe that their way of living is correct while others are perceived to live an "evil" life. As time passes on, people of different parts of the world become so fixated on their customs and traditions that they become even more intolerable of other ways of living.

"Our way is the only way!" are statements which some people proclaim in some countries.

"Kill the infidels!" Proclaim people in other countries who disagree.

All-in-all, people are drifting further away from interpersonal relationships, attitudes and values though their customs, traditions, intolerance, and religious beliefs. This is because rather than being taught to accept each other truly as people connected to each other, we are continuously led to believe that we are separate. How ironic that in some religions, we still maintain a violent attitude and behavior. People still retain the notion of "killing" or "exterminating" things and people they don't like or disagree with. A good Buddhist teaching called the Eight Fold Noble Path gives mankind a few things to ponder:

Eight Fold Noble Path

1. Right View	Wisdom
2. Right Intention	
3. Right Speech	
4. Right Action	Ethical Conduct
5. Right Livelihood	
6. Right Effort	
7. Right Mindfulness	Mental Development
8. Right Concentration	

This path is extremely difficult to follow.[xvii] Keeping a pure mind is not a simple matter. Jesus described the path to Heaven as "straight and narrow." Imagine travelling down the path to the bottom of the ravine in the Grand Canyon on a very narrow path. One wrong slip of the foot can be very disastrous – so dangerous that it might even take your life.

If we fail to keep a pure heart and fill ourselves with violence and revenge, people are capable of carrying out acts of hatred whether through the use of guns, or the stroke of a pen, or physical violence. This is totally contrary to what religious masters have taught us. The process has become so convoluted and corrupted that one will have to remove layers upon layers to find out what the real truth really is (was). People are learning lessons based on second, third or more hand, teachings which have been filtered down through multiple generations.

Take the Bible for instance -- proclaimed to be "God's Word." But in actuality, the most ancient scrolls containing "God's Word," has been transcribed by scribes in ancient times which and edited by many scholars. Not that I'm saying that they have done a terrible job of this, but there is one human flaw in this process. Passing information down from generation to generation can be subject to different interpretations – sometimes so dramatic that the original message itself would be totally different than the current modern day message!

A Classic Telephone Exercise

If you doubt this process, get a group of people together and form a circle. Have the leader start a message by telling it just to the next person – all verbal, no writing. That person tells the same message to the person next to him/her. When the message travels full circle, have the last person reveal the "same" message. Then compare to see differences in the original message.

In the new world to come, there will be no need for worldly religions as we currently know of them today. In order for man to move in the right direction, religions will find commonality amongst themselves and shed their differences. This must occur before governments of the world begin to change towards bringing people together towards oneness. Some countries like to say that there should be a separation of government and religion – this is a false assumption. Religions in every nation, have played a major role in influencing governmental policy. Religion can play a major role in bringing about peace, tranquility and equality in the world.

Ultimately, the world must break free of the strangle hold and corrupt influences of banks and corporations that control governments of the world who favor a minority of the world's elite. The ultimate power and control of the world must be returned to the domain of the people.

When mankind grew and divided into different nations,

spoke different languages, and moved to different parts of the planet, different religions were created by God. All of this done in the language of their respective understanding. Unfortunately, some things did not translate well. This has led to much disagreement between people in the world. Rather than viewing other lifestyles and cultures as an "alternative" or "just another way" of living, many people have become intolerant to other lifestyles. Some have forced their ways upon others through wars and colonization –other cultures which have created even more problems throughout history. Wars and fighting often broken out because of these disagreements – rooted in religious differences. Many church leaders were also sacrificed and martyred because their views often conflicted with governmental policy and dictates. Buddhist leaders, during the war in Indochina, for example, self-immolated in protest and disagreement of government actions of their nations.

No longer will religious or spiritual leaders have to sacrifice themselves for their respective beliefs because they may differ with government, other nations, or cultures. When humanity moves in the right direction, man will realize and respect each person as an individual having a divine, independent, different, intellectual being -- that each individual on Earth make up God's "grand tapestry."

Each individual will be granted the freedom to think and express him/herself freely and openly – not controlled by government or religion. *This* is God's will. Furthermore, as people begin to move towards oneness, religion will also begin to encourage this trend as it will help build bridges between nations. The Internet has already begun to do this.

Unfortunately, there are elements which are attempting to stop people from moving closer as a world community. They will, however, not succeed -- God's Will will be triumphant. The trend towards one world religion will set the stage for the realization of what has been foretold through biblical prophesies – *Jesus will return to establish his kingdom here on Earth*. Not only this, but I believe previous masters of all religions shall also return as well to create a new direction for the planet.

I call upon all Earth Angels and Light workers to join together in bringing religions of the world to dialogue. To serve as guiding lights in helping them find common ground and prepare the way for nations of the world to come together as one. To unite the people of the world by establishing a unified high standard of living that will ensure that poverty, homelessness, and starvation is forever eliminated from this planet and that people will adjust to a greater appreciation for the environment, God and other life forms through the realization that human beings are connected with the rest of this Earth.

Religions will return to their basic fundamental foundations and realize that they were all founded by one Creator. He has been called by many names, but commonly He is known throughout the world as, *God*. As angels on Earth join in this effort, so shall their efforts be joined by angelic beings from Heaven which will ultimately shine and illuminate the path towards love and tranquility. Wars and violence will forever cease when God truly establishes His will on Earth. Our mission, therefore, is to prepare the people of Earth for that moment which will soon come. No, there will be no destruction or violent end of the planet as people have sought to instill fear in the minds of many in the days of "Armageddon."

As I mentioned before, Buddhists say, "everything is impermanent." Forgive me, but this also includes religions of the world. Religions will also eventually see their end. But it will not be a sad ending – it will be a rebirth! As people come together as one, religions will also come to the realization that they too are actually one. Once this is realized, then people can move to influence changes in their governments, peacefully, towards unifying the world.

CHAPTER 16
RACE AND HUMAN RELATIONS

Because we have always been taught that we are separate and different from each other, our views and perspectives on race and human relations have been historically impacted. In Biblical times, for example, when a certain group of people went to battle against another group, there were illustrations of the "little people" versus the "giants." Truthfully, the Bible didn't help matters when it tells the story of Cain killing Abel in the field (Genesis 4:8). That only started a myriad of human relations problems that were compounded throughout history. However, in the New Testament, the Bible reveals excellent examples of love towards mankind with the ultimate example of Jesus laying down his life for the sins of man on the cross – the ultimate love for humanity.

Race relations have historically been an issue and continue to be a struggle in modern day civilizations. There are countless examples of how one race had exerted its dominance over other races. In ancient Biblical times, there is the example of the Egyptian domination over the Hebrew slaves. Not to pick on the people of Jewish faith, but there was the Roman Empire who dominated much of Europe and the Middle East which just so happened to include the lands where the Jewish people dwelt.

Moving on in history, there were the European colonists in early America who showed their dominance by owning African slaves. Even at the end of slavery, problems with race relations continued well into the 20th and 21st centuries. America was not alone in its problems with racial relations. The nation of Israel had their fair share of problems with the Muslims that dwelled in their land. The nation of Russia continues to have sporadic problems with ethnic groups of people residing within their borders.

Some problems have risen to critical heights when nations went to war because of their actions against targeted groups of people. For example, the German dominance and occupation of European countries during World War II have caused many Jews and Roma their lives in, perhaps, the greatest holocaust of mankind, next to the tragedies in Armenia and Rwanda.

All of this can be traced back to the story of the Tower of Babel (Genesis 11:1-9) when people suddenly spoke in different languages and scattered over the face of the Earth. At the time the Tower of Babel was being built, God punished man for building an edifice upwards towards the heavens. This is when He created different languages upon the world to bring about confusion. It was perhaps at this juncture where man began to distrust other people. Why? Misunderstanding each other? Who knows? After all, at that point, there really was no effective means of translating languages besides the fact that each unique group of people separated into their own ways – into the four corners of the world. Borders were created, walls were built. Everything was done to keep people separated. And thus, this is how mankind has always been taught to behave – separated and different from each other – conditioned to treat and approach each other with a degree of suspicion (i.e., "friend" or "foe"). It was bad enough that man had already learned how to kill and murder his own kind. Being forced to speak different languages and live under different life-styles and cultures only compounded the issue of separation. Yes, man has attempted to build bridges of peace. But these actions were always done wearing a cloak of suspicion – each side hiding something behind their backs.

When human beings were created, they were created totally naked. Perhaps at that time, human relations were much better. Why? They each had nothing to hide. God gave Adam and Eve articles of clothing to protect themselves from the elements. When they were expelled from paradise, they probably did not need clothing because the climate was perfect 24/7. Clothing, therefore, was provided to protect them from the elements. Some have theorized that God, when he expelled Adam and Eve from Eden, instilled a sense of shame at that point. Although I was not there when the Bible was edited, I believe this to be an addition of man in order to control people's mind. I think the human form is still pleasing to God in its natural form and He doesn't care if it is clothed or not.

On the other hand, when you're evolving from another creature from the sea, or being created using a model from another creature, such as an ape, monkey, chimpanzee, or gorilla, the lowest priority on a Creator's mind would be putting a costume on his creations and probably more concerned that His creation is working or "operating" properly and successfully.

The debate between creationism and evolution has also created a great divide among many people. In my mind, *drop the issue--* it's not important. The fact of the matter is, we are all here as human beings. How we came here to Earth is unimportant. Besides, the fact is, neither side has been able to sufficiently prove beyond a reasonable doubt the argument for creationism or evolution using based on *FACTUAL and SATISFACTORY EVIDENCE.* Although, there is reasonable evidence showing that mankind *has evolved* from a particular tribe of people originating from a region now known as East Africa.[xviii] The important matter is that man moves on to improve race and human relations and forget about the past. There remains a lot of work to be done. We've become so engrossed as to where, how and when we came here to Earth that we often neglect to work towards building better relations between ourselves. We let trivial matters such as creationism and evolution divide us rather than concentrating on more important issues as building better bridges, accepting each other's views and coming closer together as human beings. Historically, we would much rather focus on matters that polarize us rather than focusing on ways that would bring us closer together.

All humans have metallic elements in their physical bodies. This was by design. We have been created from elements from various Earth's composition which contained metallic elements. Some of these metals would naturally create an anti-magnetic field which would cause a polarity between human beings. This would cause a natural separation and feeling of "suspicion" to a very minute degree. The polarity of human relationships is enhanced by the mind for, it creates false barriers that dictate to an individual what is acceptable, and what is unacceptable. Many consider this as the "human defense mechanism." It is a way for an individual to defend him/herself. Some say it's a natural instinct. Whatever it would be called, the mind is so unique that it has the capability of controlling this process depending on how it is "programmed." This programming is often influenced through societal influences such as family, friends, community, educational, and religious or non-religious influences.

When there are different standards in the world, the minds are programmed differently. Some are programmed more successfully than others. This is why there is a large discrepancy in educational standards and performance. I will talk about this matter later on in the vision for education. But as it pertains to race and human relations, it also affects the way people behave. Some of this is demonstrated through the quality of cities and communities which tend to be better of some countries than in others that dwell in poverty and desolation. Don't just observe the discrepancies in the world, take a look at those that exist within metropolitan areas also. In many cities, some areas are better developed than others, all within the same municipal limits.

The world has yet to adopt a unified high quality standard for Earth. In many countries, poorer countries experience high rates of unemployment and poor housing while governments do very little to rectify their people's needs. In most of the world, there is a significant imbalance between the "have's" and "have-not's." The poor of the world is continuing to increase while a very small percentage of the population appears to be living well off of other people's toils and efforts. This is not new, however. Historically, there are many illustrations of a small group of people exerting their dominance over a poorer group of people (i.e., kings and royalty versus peasants and slaves). In modern times, some people appear to have gained considerably more wealth at the expense of others.

Some say it's too expensive to care for the homeless or

to solve the problems of poverty or hunger. These would only come from people whom are too concerned about protecting their own ways of living. Typically, if it were up to them, the people in distress should rather be exterminated or eliminated from Earth rather than allowed to continue to live on the face of the planet. *Human life is valuable and precious.* I say, rid the world of money and currency – it's easier than ridding the world of human life. Every human has the inherent right to live. No one has the right to deny another person from living.

No man has the right to assert supreme authority over another for we all were created equally. We were born into this world, naked with nothing; so shall we depart from this planet with nothing. "The greatest among you will be your *servant.*" (Matthew 23:11). Whereas people who toil on the farms, maintain buildings, and work in the factories should be respected equally as with office workers, government leaders and elected officials. You should all be servants towards each other with equal salaries. The problem is, in many countries, people have placed themselves on pedestals. This has given them a false notion that their positions are more superior then others. They give themselves more benefits and privileges over people who have really labored more than they do.

Remove the pedestals of society and level the playing field. Consider yourselves as all servants – everyone just as important as the highest person in the country. In other words, the persons maintaining the toilets are respected equally as much and the head of a company. The only difference is, you are all using different skills and parts of your physical bodies. Because you are blessed with a better education than another, there is no excuse for treating other humans with lesser educational backgrounds inferior to you.

Nevertheless, your job, whether it be a white or blue collar position, is equal in God's eyes. Serve one another and see each other as a human being with each individual mutually respected and appreciated.

Government leaders should not wield their powers and authorities over the will of their peoples. If the will of the people demands change, then so be it. Governments should quietly and peacefully step aside and bow to the people's will and desires and not exert power through force and military might just because they have these resources at their command. Ultimately, the power of the people will be victorious and will topple any form of regime. The collective will of the people is only God's way of creating change. Some governmental leaders may be blind to this because they are too focused on their own agenda and refuse to change. Everything changes in the world. The existence of governments is no exception to this universal law. Change may come gradually, or it may happen instantaneously -- this *is* the force of God. Man has ultimately no control over these forces despite his technological and military might. What takes man months or even years to build can quickly be destroyed in a matter of minutes or seconds by God even with the best made plans. Take the destructive forces of an earthquake or hurricane for example that can level a city in a matter of minutes that took years to build.

Therefore, do not resist change. Live and adjust to change for these happen daily, hourly, by the minute. Man has historically been conditioned that he was forever immunized to change even to the point where minds have become calloused. Therefore, the way people behave towards race and human relations have essentially remained the same since the beginning of man – only that the problem has become progressively worse. Masters have come to this Earth to teach us how to change our behavior. But like children, we have been stubborn in changing by not listening. We have either misinterpreted their teachings or have totally rejected them.

Face it, as a people of modern times trying to move forward in the right direction, we have a lot to unravel in terms of bad behavior. People have inherited a lot of bad traits that were handed down to them through generations. Breaking these habits will probably take the next few generations before humanity can actually take steps to move in the right direction.

First, people will need to understand the bad behaviors that humans have developed over history and begin to make changes towards improving human relations and bridging racial divide. Don't just talk about doing so – but make constructive efforts to move closer together as one through mutual respect, understanding, and tolerance. Not only among your immediate neighbors in your communities, but also among your nations, across your borders and oceans with other nations. To some respects, the Internet -- through social networking -- has done a successful job in building part of this bridge on a virtual level. We must take steps to do this on a physical and emotional level as well. Governments should not create barriers in preventing this to occur. It should encourage "immigration reform" in a positive aspect of inviting people in – not in the converse aspect of keeping people "out."

Good human relations begin in the home. Throughout the world, there are many families who suffer from the misfortunes of broken relationships between husband and wife, parents, relatives and close loved ones. Learning how to create good human relations starts at an early age with parents serving as the example. It does not bode well when the husband dominates the wife by spousal abuse, beating, rape, and torture in the presence of their children. This only plants seeds which only culminates in bad behavior later on – a domino effect if you will.

Marriage should be an equal partnership where both man and woman support each other in love. It takes a lot of work. Man was not made to be domineering over woman, nor vice versa. No one human was made to "own" another human. All humans were created to be free from any bondage. Live life freely and express this freedom to your children. If you demonstrate dominance through violence and a "superiority complex" over your spouse, this will be reflected through your children, who, in turn will often magnify your actions by doing the same to other innocent children through actions such as "bullying."

In the United States, for example, bullying incidents are on the rise. Innocent children take their lives because they cannot handle the harsh abuse due to the psychological injuries suffered at the hands of other children. Yet, many school districts, communities, and local governments lack policies to prevent and enforce the protection of innocent children against such abuse. The ignorance of taking such action is because the people in power and authority have probably been bullies themselves and often look the other way when children often act in such a manner. There is no excuse for such behavior. Parents, educators, and government leaders must be held accountable for the actions of children who act with criminal-like behaviors. To let them continue to act in such a fashion will only escalate into behaviors that will become increasingly worse and more difficult to correct when they (the children) become adults. Society cannot turn blind eye to this matter. In the new world, good human relations will be part of educational curricula in the world.

Improving human relations not only pertains to just ones family members if they are perceived as "normal" or "straight." Improving human relations also means improving relations with *all* whom man has falsely categorized into "inferior categories." Such as gays, lesbians, bisexuals, transsexuals, transgenders, bi-(multi-)racial, foreign nationalities and cultures, races, or any other class of people that are considered "out of the ordinary." To God, there is no "out of the ordinary." Everyone is *human* in the eyes of God. He does not discriminate. Only man and religion has done a pathetic job in creating such labels. Centuries of bad habits and traditions must be reversed. They can be reversed, but man must take the initiative of reversing attitudes and behavior before he can begin to move forward in the right direction. For those who refuse to change, they will be left behind – stuck in quicksand. The new world will demand tolerance and openness from each and every individual regardless of national origin, culture or religious background.

The underlying essence of a marriage is love and mutual respect. Love knows no boundaries whether it be between a man and a woman, or between two men, or two women. The issues and struggle is a fight for equal opportunities granted to the "traditional institution of marriage" which in itself still has a lot of problems in itself. Many people argue for the sacredness of marriage between only a man and a woman. Yet, problems of these arrangements scar its sanctity -- such as divorce; separation of couples; spousal abuse; murder and homicide; child abuse; wife beatings; etc. All of these just for the benefits of being married to one another such as tax benefits, survivor's benefits, etc.

The "institution of marriage" still has a long way to go before it can become an "ideal institution" sanctioned by either religion or the courts. In order to qualify for a marriage license, couples should not only undergo the traditional spiritual counseling, but both should seek anger management courses, psychological evaluation, financial counseling including money management and budgeting, and a full course covering, the ramifications of being married and the responsibilities of doing so. These issues customarily were left to the responsibility of the parents of the engaged couples, but the families no longer fulfill many of these obligations.

In fact, many marriages start off irresponsibly to begin with by spending a fortune on the wedding ceremony. Many couples take out loans and are immediately in more debt before they even start their families, just for the sake of providing the illusion of a "royal wedding" -- something that many families cannot afford to do. Rather than spent money wisely and budgeting the funds for a practical wedding ceremony and celebration, couples often spend an extravagant amount. Here too, the institution of marriage has fallen victim to the profit making wedding industry. Many fall victim to their prey. Many times, it's not for the sake of "love," rather it's for "pay back," or "social obligations." Then too, a lot of money is invested just to "impress others."

In the new world, one of the old practices that will no longer be tolerated is the practice of torture, rape, and physical beatings. This is the greatest violation against an individual's right to a dignified living. No matter what position a person is in, or what capacity of authority a person represents, the individual does not have the license to abuse another person's body for the soul purpose of "extracting" information from someone else by force -- especially if such brutal methods cause physical harm, emotional damage, and even death. No matter if it is an agent of a federal or national government, or a local municipal government (i.e. the police), these persons should be held accountable for their actions for crimes against humanity, no matter what country they dwell in. Furthermore, all those associated with these crimes should be held equally accountable for subscribing to, and supporting such brutal actions against mankind. If, by chance, these include leaders of nations, they, too, should be held equally accountable for these crimes, and brought to justice in a universal court of law. No nation should be exempt or given special courtesies from the laws that protect humanity. These laws should be enforced equally throughout the entire world.

Likewise, women must also be given equal protection against men who perform acts of aggression and who chastise them as "objects" or "property." Women should not be perceived as "lesser" or "inferior" species of the human race, but must be considered as equals. Women are created to be equally compatible with men – in loving partnership – not one in dominance over the other. Many times, journalists cover stories where women in the world are tragically beaten (sometimes to death) for infidelity by their husbands. Then, there are other accounts where husbands are given light sentences for cheating on their spouses. Laws in the world typically favor men. There needs to be an legal balance where men and women are provided with equal justice. Mankind must end its ancient ways of human relationships between men and women and begin to view each other as equal human beings. If there is to be balance in the world, it must begin with a balance between men and women. Both sexes have equal strengths – and on the flip side of the coin, equal weaknesses. Both sides were designed to support each other – not tear each other apart. Therefore, choose your mate carefully and wisely whether it would be of the opposite sex, or the same sex.

To improve human and racial relations among nations,

end the practice of exporting weapons and armament among yourselves. "What goes around, comes around." Learn your lessons from the past! Convert your offensive militaries into forces of peace. Export peaceful cadres of educators, artisans, musicians, physicians, and builders of life – not forces that destroy civilizations, and create unbearable misery to humanity. Create a high standard of living and apply it to the entire world – not just certain segments of the world's elite. Build a world of equality and opportunity for all.

CHAPTER 17
ENERGY

The first cave dwellers found ways of keeping themselves warm by starting a fire. This was the earliest form of "home heating." Man has since made remarkable improvements since those days. Now, instead of wood to heat the house, we can use natural gas, oil, coal, solar, hydroelectric and atomic energy to heat a dwelling. By and large, the use of energy resources has been used for peaceful purposes.

However, historically, countries have been known to have gone to war because they lacked certain resources that other nations had. Oil, for example, is one resource which some areas had a plentiful supply of and others lacked. In some cases, politics were used to gain access to these resources, either by negotiation with other governments, or by force through military action. If the later options were taken, often, innocent lives were sacrificed in order to gain access to these resources. Occasionally, the reason for going to war was fabricated in order to gain access to these resources.

Yet, other wars and disagreements over energy resources

were created over fears and paranoia. Nuclear energy, for example, remains a controversial issue in the world. Some countries have more nuclear weapons on hand to destroy the planet ten-times over. Smaller countries are yet coming around to developing their own nuclear arsenals. Even though there may be a reason to use nuclear energy for peaceful purposes, there is the sinister side of nuclear energy which destroys man. The two biggest examples are its use in Hiroshima and Nagasaki during World War II. Two major cities in Japan were vaporized at the hands of the United States which triggered a major nuclear arms race in the world – mass hysteria. It has become so bad, that man cannot reverse its insatiable appetite for nuclear arms. Yet, these countries are very paranoid and skittish when a smaller nation researches nuclear energy for "peaceful intent" saying that if the materials fall into the wrong hands, it would be very deadly to "peaceful nations."

The best solution to this entire dilemma is to rid the world of its entire nuclear arsenal – everyone, large and small nations alike. Nuclear weapons only serve one purpose – to destroy humanity. It would all be due to the stubbornness and arrogance of man's refusal to destroy the nuclear weapons of the world that will destroy mankind unless he begins to step forward in the right direction and shed these things that do not serve humanity well – this includes nuclear weapons. Maybe they'll serve their purpose pointed outward into space towards incoming asteroids. But as long as they are targeted at cities, they serve no purpose. Look at the destructive damage nuclear energy itself, unharnessed, has on marine life in the oceans.

Man will also have to better manage the resources of the Earth. In some cases, he's depleted all of Earth's energy's resources in order for his own gain. And while over consuming these resources, he has been very slow to develop new alternative resources. Man has a continual behavior of "passing the buck." That is, he repeatedly leaves things to be learned for the "next generation." Man should always be helping future generations by looking forward – not continuously living in the "present" with "old traditions" and "values." This is why man has yet to make remarkable progress.

When it comes to improving on energy resources, politics also serve as a barrier towards progress. Lawmakers, not educated about technology or science, often create policies and laws which prohibit or limit progress, funding, and resources and frequently block major projects that would improve new energy resources. Man has always assumed that resources were plentiful and that they would last forever.

Earth was made only for temporary storage. If managed wisely, resources can last for generations. But through arrogance, he has built machinery and man-made objects that waste a lot of Earth's resources. Much of Earth's supply will not be enough to provide for future generations because previous generations have greedily consumed existing supplies.

Take automobiles, for example. Rather than building vehicles that would run on mere tablespoons of gasoline, cars continue to be built that would consume gallons of gasoline. Man has yet to learn how to conserve the natural energy resources of the Earth. By harnessing alternative forms of energy such as wind, hydroelectric, geothermal, biofuels, solar, and renewable energy such as those which may be supplied by materials such as industrial hemp and bagasse. Countries are too concerned about saving corporations and their profits rather than prolonging and saving the resources of the world. Sadly, the latter dwindle while man tries to maximize profits often while limiting supplies to the rest of the world.

By and large, man has proven himself to be a very poor manager of Earth's resources and the environment. Conservation efforts that are taken to save Earth's environment are often squashed through political channels in favor of supporting profit-making polluting manufacturing and production companies. All this while harming not only the environment, but creating an unhealthful ecosystem for the people. A country full of sick people cannot support the cause of a nation. But when the needs of the people are placed in a lower priority than profits, then the entire country suffers. The nation's economy declines, the morale of the people also weakens and there is a general disconnect with government and its citizens.

In January of 2011, this was true in the Arab countries of the Middle East where people said enough was enough. Poor unemployed people and students rose against their governments in protest during the "Arab Spring" and demanded better living conditions.

Masters of the world have often emphasized to put people first and foremost. Then everything will fall into place. Many governments have failed to adhere to this advice. Consequently, many governments have been toppled and many are about ready to be overthrown -- all because the energy of the people is stronger than any government.

Yes, we know more commonly about Earth's energy resource such as oil, wind, solar, electricity, etc. But we often neglect about another resource which is often mismanaged – *human energy*. When human energy is high, people are productive and contribute to society. When they are demoralized, they are unmotivated and cannot contribute well to the efforts of a nation. Governments at all levels must learn to keep the morale of their people consistently high by continuously keeping their energies high. Any dip in their energy levels, and productivity is certain to drop and attitudes towards leaders become very negative. In some cases, even hostile. Governments must also ensure the health and well-being of its population by ensuring proper healthcare for all as a right for every person. And by supplying proper nutrition with healthy, organic and affordable food – not manufactured by corporations instilling pesticides in vegetables, farm products and processed food products which are harmful to human consumption, yet alone, laboratory animals.

Human energy has a profound impact on the entire world's productivity. If some parts of the world suffer from low energy levels, then that part of the world's productivity is also very low. Some of this is due to the negative energy emitted by their governments. Many government leaders are not capable of facilitating high energy levels. In fact, most leaders often create negative energy. If this be the case, then it is time to replace your government representatives. I encourage peaceful means of transitioning your leadership, for the voice of the people is much more powerful than any governmental force. This has been demonstrated by the people of Egypt during their massive demonstrations for change in 2011 which then encouraged people of other Middle Eastern nations such as Egypt and Libya to do the same.

People often forget that each individual *is energy*. Each human being is made up of a complex series of atoms and molecules, arranged so that we each have our own unique individuality. But because we have similar compositions that make up elements of other life forms not only on Earth, but also in the universe, we often forget the fact that we all are connected to every element in God's creation. We are interdependent on other life forms for our survival. Yet, man has already destroyed many life forms on Earth leading to the destruction of his own kind.

Many artists through the creation of movies, books, and art forms have taught us valuable lessons of the importance of connectivity. Yet, man continues to disregard these lessons. He continues to destroy elements of the Earth through pollution and mismanagement of the planet's resources. A song in the popular Disney movie, the *Lion King,* it talks about the "Circle of Life." I might add that man must learn how to live with the "Balance of Life" also. Though his actions and misdeeds, he has caused a great imbalance of life on Earth. One example of this is our problem with global warming and the extinction of wildlife.

God delegated dominion of Earth to man.[xix] But this responsibility was to ensure that life is sustained and flourishes on Earth – not to be controlled in the fashion as some government leaders do when passing legislation based on religious beliefs practically governing sexual behavior and controlling population growth. The management of life was intended to be a natural process, not a superficial process of controlling something that is a natural behavior. After all, the matter of reproduction occurs naturally in other animal life forms without the need for man-made intervention. That is, dogs, cats, elephants, lions, tigers, horses, cows, birds, reptiles, fishes, and other life forms mate naturally. So should man be allowed to mate naturally without the interference of other men dictating when or when not to mate. This is over control of human energy – something that occurs naturally. Some within the species do have over-active sex drives. These behaviors must be recognized and managed humanely.

When it comes to energy, man must recognize that there are many forms of energy at his disposal – not just oil, coal, electricity, solar, and biofuels. The over-use of certain energy forms will quickly deplete Earth's available supplies. Man must learn how to use a wide variety of energy forms that are available and shed interferences that prohibit him from doing so – particularly beliefs and attitudes related to profits, religion, and politics. These anchors prohibit mankind from progressing forward into exploring other forms of available energy and often restrict the kinds of energy available to mankind. When politics are involved, the progression of exploring for other forms of energy are inhibited and often blocked in favor of special interests. This does not serve the citizens well – particularly when Earth's supply of existing energy resources are being depleted rapidly. Man must take his blinders off and rapidly move forward towards alternative forms of energy and shed old values, practices, policies, and behaviors.

Talking about energy in general, man must find ways to harness all types of energy so that they are friendly to life and also the environment.

Through chemical engineering, we have found ways to develop products that are harmful to health and toxic to the environment. Many of the chemicals end up in drinking water. Government officials often claim that they are at "safe levels" for consumption. In reality, even the smallest amount of these chemicals is not safe. Man was not made to ingest these chemicals. Life is delicate and precious. The smallest trace of toxic chemicals can cause serious health effects such as cancer, which has been a problem of man for decades. This was not a major factor in the days of Adam and Eve. But not only has man learned of ways to put chemicals in water, but also in foods, soil, and animal products. These are presently causing serious health issues.

Energy in chemistry is only one area. Electrical engineering is also another area which is also a major concern causing harm to life on Earth. The invention of the microwave as benefitted man in some ways, but has come at a cost. The advent of cell phones has brought people together tremendously. However, the health issues of the brain and associated organs have also risen during the advent of the microwave. Life forms are constantly being bombarded with radio waves created not only by radio itself, but also by microwave towers, television, ultraviolet, and other forms of invisible radio waves that constantly pass through one's body. This technology has brought billions of dollars to corporations. But are people paying a price with their lives?

There is also another form of energy which is related to lifestyles. I shall talk about this form in that chapter later on.

CHAPTER 18
WORLD EQUALITY

S ince the creation of man, the world has never been equal. I cannot say this for sure because I was not around during the time of Adam and Eve, but reading the story of the couple, it seems like Adam didn't consider Eve as an equal. Or, the stories were edited to appear that Adam had a more dominant role over his partner. But as mankind evolved, the species treated each other differently. There were definite splits, a loss of respect for each other, and the matter has been compounded as nations were created, thus creating further divisions between people. The introduction of currencies also did not help the matter of equality either. There have always been varying degrees of inequality.

So is the assumption that men are created equal really true? Assuming that the color of one's skin is not an issue, then, it is absolutely true that all humans are created – physically – equal, the same. Each has different characteristics, traits, and genetic differences. But, the process is generally the same if delivered naturally. Some have been born by artificial influences or processes. But by and large, we all have been born from an egg and a sperm. Unfortunately, the mind filters and segregates individuals into "classes" such as color, sex, race, age, etc. It cannot just settle on the fact that we are all born as humans with identical characteristics and similarities. It is the differences, preferences, likes and dislikes that often lead men into trouble, disagreements – some violently, others non-violently.

It is these degrees of inequality where some humans consider themselves more privileged than others. Some tend to cluster in greater groups than others (i.e. nations). Some nations exert their dominance over other nations, thus the existence of some nations that are supremely rich and powerful over other nations who are exactly the opposite – poor, starving, and illiterate. Even in the more affluent nations, there are disparities of ultra-rich and poor.

The world, must address the drastic discrepancies between rich and poor, and begin to work towards equality for all – an equitable society where wealth and resources are distributed fairly and equally. Mankind must eliminate the barriers that purposely limit resources to the masses. Resources of the world were meant to be managed, not controlled for profit. God gave man dominion over the Earth to manage its resources, without currency or money. Man took it upon himself to apply money to these resources in order to limit supplies. Money was never part of God's plan, for currency causes problems – especially inequality and human grief, when money itself is limited to the people, causing high rates of unemployment, starvation, homelessness and poverty.

To date, there remains a disparity of equal pay between men and women. Women are continued to be paid much less than men for equal work. In fact, in many cases, women do more work than men, but are paid considerably less than their male counterparts. This book is about just moving humankind in the right direction. Therefore, both men and women must move together, equally. The world must address the disparity of pay between men and women and learn how to pay women equally with men. Of course, the elimination of currencies would solve this riddle all together.

In the world, there also exist an enormous disparity between rich countries and poor. This must be addressed also. The world must adapt to a unified standard of living throughout the planet where all countries are on an equal level. Some countries are practically treated as slaves to other nations. This need not be so. This behavior should be considered as crimes against humanity. Richer nations should not pillage the resources of a poor nation without due compensation.

CHAPTER 19
LABOR & EMPLOYMENT

In ancient times, man kept himself occupied with a craft, a trade, or a special skill which typically traded for other goods or services. Much of the time, this was done without the exchange of money. Also, he did this without the fear of being laid off because "companies" could no longer afford to keep him employed. Largely because large companies did not exist in ancient times. An occupation was a way of satisfying the creativity of the "child-self." The workplace was typically the "adult playground." It was a place for the adult to expend the "child energy" still within the person.

In modern times, this "playground" has rapidly diminished in favor of profit making corporations which had exported many jobs from the United States overseas in what was termed as "globalization." Although this has brought the world closer together, this has also displaced many Americans from their homes and families. It was also detrimental to the individual. The loss of jobs denied them their "adult playgrounds." As many became unemployed, a good portion of the them also became homeless. Their "playground" soon became the streets of metropolitan cities and suburbs of America.

Yet, employees are expected to survive on their own, often with only thirty-days unemployment assistance from the companies, 26 weeks California Employment Development Department Department Unemployment Insurance, plus 37 week Federal extension. When this assistance is depleted, and no other forms of income is available, the individual's credit ratings are ruined for life through no fault of their own but blame can be placed on an unforgiving society. A society that blames an individual for losing his or her job when it was really the company's problem for mismanaging its resources. But no, it doesn't hold corporations accountable, rather it holds individuals accountable for not being able to find jobs. It is the fault of a system which considers workers as highly expendable as material objects, rather than members of a forgiving society. A society that is dictated by the operations of computers, rather than being over-ridden by human intervention.

The world must find a means of keeping every able-bodied person occupied, yes even those considered as "senior citizens" or the "elderly." All too often, when people reach a certain age in life, they are expected to retire. In chapter 22 on education, I will elaborate on how the elderly can play a more dynamic role in the educational process.

In many countries around the turn of the 20th Century, labor unions were organized because of management's little regard for the care and wellbeing of its employees. Few benefits were offered, working conditions were highly risky, and many workers suffered major illnesses associated as a consequence of their jobs. Unions served as their advocates in the workplace.

In recent times, the unions' image has been tarnished.

Many have blamed them for increasing employment costs, raising healthcare costs and benefits, corruption, not defending workers' rights, and a myriad of other issues. Management, on the other hand has been notorious for dipping into employee retirement funds, getting paid higher salaries than the President of the United States, and corruption. Government, depending on the political party in power, has been attempting to destroy unions altogether. In one state, it had been successful by unlawful legislative procedures such as conducting business behind closed doors. [xx] A scenario, in most cases, which is highly unethical, and in many cases, highly illegal. Yet, it was done regardless of the law.

If management in businesses acted more responsibly towards their employees, then there wouldn't be the necessity for unionization in the first place. Unions, afterall, were meant to ensure that employees were treated humanely with their safety ensured, a fair work week with a living wage or salary, and to have a voice in the company through elected representation.

If companies followed the basic principles of democracy and freedom of speech, these practices would have been unnecessary. Employees would have been treated more humanely rather than like animals, slaves, or property. However, managers have preferred to consider themselves as elite by separating themselves into a special group in their company rather than considering themselves as equals working for a common cause. In many companies, they've instilled the "master-slave" environment and mentality. To date, this concept is still practiced in many companies. Hence, when it comes to downsizing and cutbacks, it is typically the lower level employees that are the first to be laid off – not the people who typically earn the most money in the company, the executives. Yet, bad management practices are often rewarded by the stockholders – they are often retained in their leadership positions rather than being terminated.

People responsible for steering a ship into an iceberg should be terminated from their positions, not retained. It is the blindness of these people who originally wasted a lot of company money and energy to begin with. The problem is, rather than promoting managers from within, companies hire executives externally. Many do not know anything about the company nor its personnel and are often blind and knows less of company polices, operations and history. They are often relied to take the company in a "new direction." But often, they lead a company in the wrong direction due to their lack of experience with the company. Where there should be more oversight in government, there also should be more oversight in corporations. Yet the problem is, corporations and government are scratching each other's back. There is absolutely no oversight anywhere. Then the citizens wonder why the country has an economic meltdown. Why is there are such a huge loss of jobs in a country and no one seems to care? Government is unresponsible to the needs of its citizens, banks refuse to loan money to the people, and corporations do not provide enough jobs for the people. Again, we have this little issue about money again.

But getting back to the issue of keeping everyone occupied, there is a simple importance in doing so. Whenever there were spikes in the population, such as "baby booms," it was typically during times of economic downturns. Why? Because people had nothing better to do than to repopulate the nation. Look at poorer nations where there are high levels of unemployment and you will find areas of overpopulation. So the answer is not to control population growth by genocide, war, and birth control. Put your people back to work and keep them occupied.

CHAPTER 20
LIFE STYLES

One cannot argue that life styles in the world are dramatically different in various parts of the world. In many respects, this is good. This has offered a wide variety of different, unique, and interesting cultures, traditions and customs. One cannot say that one life style is right while another is wrong. These are just different ways of living.

What needs to be addressed are the life styles between the extremely rich, and extremely poor. Some nations are extremely well-to-do while others live in absolute poverty. The standard of living must be raised for all parts of the world in order for mankind to move forward in the right direction. Man has historically separated himself into groups – economic classes. Then, in some countries always preached that "men were created equal" but never practiced that concept. India, for example, never claimed to this statement, for in their country, there always existed various economic classes of highly rich people, and extremely poor – a caste system. In America, there is the very same class structure as in many other countries. In several countries, some are so well off, that they are put on pedestals by their people through what they would refer to as "royal families" or "nobility." In America, there are the very wealthy or affluent such as millionaires and billionaires.

For the Kingdom of Heaven to be established on Earth, there needs to be only one class of people – one level playing field where everyone is entitled to the exact same opportunities of abundance – no more, no less. This applies throughout the entire world – one nation not superior to another, but all nations as equals.

Furthermore, for the term, "Men are created equally," to truly become a reality, this must include everyone, every being, regardless of race, gender, religion, and sexual orientation, without regard to prejudice, discrimination and hatred. Yes, this also includes gays, lesbians, bisexuals, and transgender. Those of religious faiths would claim these people to be an "abomination." God loves these people as he loves everyone else.

These people *are humans* – made up of the same atoms, molecules, and protons like all other human beings. I am not a physicist, scientist, or physician. But there are medical facts and evidence supporting their sexual attraction to each other of the same. My personal belief is that the concept is so complex and fascinating that I am not even going to try to attempt to explain it in this book. In simple terms, like attracts like (i.e. like molecules attract like molecules). It is not a matter of "choice" as some people would have us believe. You can't change this way of living. The principle is the exact same as being born either a boy or a girl, brown or blue eyes, we all have our differences – each person was born uniquely this way. It is genetically engrained in the individual. And, we all possess genetic defects whether we are straight or not. So, embrace them, love them, and care for them as fellow human beings.

For religious believers to claim that LGBT's are "messed up," I invite them to each undergo a genetic study and find out how many genetic defects they each possess. Whether we're straight or not, *we all carry genetic defects*. We all are not perfect. May only he who is absolutely genetically perfect cast the first stone; otherwise, bridle your tongues and remain in silence, speak only when you have learned how to love.

Facts now exist in modern times that did not exist when the Bible was written. There is reason to adapt to changes in this world. *God is change*. He continues to shape and reshape our lives like a clay potter, continuously forming and reforming a work of art. Fortunately, this work of art has never gone to the kiln. Our individual lives continuously improve because God continues to inspire us to make course corrections through a behavioral change or event. We may find that our tastes and preferences change. Things that we have disliked as children suddenly become favorites in adulthood. Gradually our eyes open up to see and appreciate the greatness of everything in the entire world including art, culture, science and yes, technology. For when an individual begins to think on a higher level, a universal level, he is able to "connect the dots," and discover that they all lead to a higher source. Some call this entity, "God." Others have other names for Him. Yet others know that there is a higher influence, but do not recognize the existence at all. This is all well. These are only different ways of seeing the same things from different perspectives. They all lead to the same source.

This is why we have dramatically different lifestyles on Earth. When people claim that their lifestyle, values, moral and religious beliefs are the only way or that they are superior then others, they have been deceived and are totally wrong.

God has purposely created different lifestyles to offer color and variety for the world. Otherwise, the world would be mere robots, clones of the same thing. When people say that their way is the "only way," they have been blind to the fact that God has created many ways to the same destination. This is best illustrated by the many highways leading to the same destination. Some routes are more direct than others. This is, perhaps, the same with religions – some are more direct than others. God did this by design knowing that some of man's religions would fail through time and history. Like roads, some break down through time, bridges collapse because of old, worn-out material. The laws of creation only dictate that everything eventually fades away through time. After all, we do live in the physical world. As the physical body is no exception, religions are also no exception. This is why many religions of the world are experiencing so much change. *God is moving.* Unlike the words in the Bible standing still in bound text, *God is continuous motion.* Lifestyles are changing and will continue to do so. He is the living form of *energy.*

God manifests Himself through many different, unique lifestyles. Places where problems in the world develop are where one group of people insist their way of living is far superior to others and forcefully impose their ways on other people. This creates anxiety and distrust. Then people wonder why there is violence and bloodshed. Rather than letting each live their own ways, other people feel they have to impose different ways of living, this is highly disruptive to one's long standing tradition and lifestyle. So much that occasionally, it leads to war. Why break something that is God's creation and has worked for ages?

Ever since the beginning of man, we have created lifestyles to encourage privacy – things to "hide" or keep out of the view of other people. Originally, the first couple did not have anything to hide. But as life progressed, we have created lifestyles that promoted the imposition of personal values on each other – "rights" and "wrongs." People couldn't just be satisfied with just keeping their noses in their own business. They had to meddle in other people's affairs. When borders and walls were created, these elevated the levels of curiosity amongst individuals and groups of people. People became naturally concerned for what was going on, "on the other side of the fence."

If they didn't like what was going on, they would intervene. Sometimes with force (i.e. police, military, militia). Yet, if they heavily disagreed with their neighbors, they would act aggressively typically in an act of takeover in some form of war or ousting of the ruling regime.

This would not happen if the world settled on one way of living --a unified high standard of living acceptable to the entire world. The Venus Project -- Beyond Politics Poverty and War presents and interesting vision of the World website's illustrations present an interesting vision of what civilizations would look like in the future.[xxi]

CHAPTER 21
SCIENCE, TECHNOLOGY AND MEDICINE

Since the Stone Age, man has made remarkable advancements and achievements in science and technology. Railroads have connected people from coast to coast and airplanes have done wonders bridging nations together. In the Twentieth Century alone, man has put himself on the moon and successfully explored Mars through robotic landing vehicles.

In medicine, man has discovered cures for many ailments and is on the threshold of making more advancements in health care. People are now able to live longer.

Electronics have made remarkable strides particularly in computer technology. Where computers once took up the size of an entire building, computations and much more now can be done remotely in the palm of one's hand.

But with the advent of new technological advances in science and technology, there have been drawbacks often limiting their progress towards success.

First of all is the politicization of science and technology.

One way to ruin something that is beneficial for mankind is to politicize it. Though the politicization of science and technology come barriers caused by the influences of corporate business leaders, religious leaders, and politicians.

In the corporate world, business leaders who often fund medicine and technological projects exert their influence on the outcomes of these projects by controlling the funding. Rather than sufficiently funding a project which ultimately may benefit man, in general, they are more concerned about keeping their shareholders pacified. Thus, by controlling the costs, projects often get derailed and the outcomes are cut short. Business leaders are more concerned about "cutting corners" rather than seeing something to its fullest success. And when it doesn't meet expectations, projects are often scrubbed for something else. But whether a project is a success or not, executives always find a way of rewarding themselves anyway regardless if the company makes a profit or not. Somehow, there is something wrong with this picture.

So, rather than researching cures for diseases like cancer, they hold back and provide only "band-aids" or temporary remedies for these ailments just to maximize profits. Many elements that might offer cures for cancer, for example cannabis, are often subject to false or misleading information both in industry and government and are often confused with the drug form of "marijuana." Medical studies have shown that certain strains of cannabis can offer cures for cancer but have not been introduced into the medical world as a "common cure."[xxii] Largely, due to, perhaps, governmental bureaucracy and scrutiny that such drugs must undergo before they are approved for regular use.

The noted Dr. Sanjay Gupta reversed his impression of marijuana in an article appearing in CNN Health.

I traveled around the world to interview medical leaders,

149

experts, growers and patients. I spoke candidly to them, asking tough questions. What I found was stunning.

Long before I began this project, I had steadily reviewed the scientific literature on medical marijuana from the United States and thought it was fairly unimpressive. Reading these papers five years ago, it was hard to make a case for medicinal marijuana. I even wrote about this in a TIME magazine article, back in 2009, titled "Why I would Vote No on Pot."

Well, I am here to apologize.

I apologize because I didn't look hard enough, until now. I didn't look far enough. I didn't review papers from smaller labs in other countries doing some remarkable research, and I was too dismissive of the loud chorus of legitimate patients whose symptoms improved on cannabis.

Instead, I lumped them with the high-visibility malingerers, just looking to get high. I mistakenly believed the Drug Enforcement Agency listed marijuana as a schedule 1 substance because of sound scientific proof. Surely, they must have quality reasoning as to why marijuana is in the category of the most dangerous drugs that have "no accepted medicinal use and a high potential for abuse."

They didn't have the science to support that claim, and I now know that when it comes to marijuana neither of those things are true. It doesn't have a high potential for abuse, and there are very legitimate medical applications. In fact, sometimes marijuana is the only thing that works. Take the case of Charlotte Figi, who I met in Colorado. She started having seizures soon after birth. By age 3, she was having 300 a week, despite being on seven different medications. Medical marijuana has calmed her brain, limiting her seizures to 2 or 3 per month.

I have seen more patients like Charlotte first hand, spent time with them and come to the realization that it is irresponsible not to provide the best care we can as a medical community, care that could involve marijuana.

We have been terribly and systematically misled for nearly 70 years in the United States, and I apologize for my own role in that.[xxiii]

Religious leaders have often thrown road blocks into advancement in medicine by inserting their religious beliefs that whatever is being done in medicine or science is contrary to their doctrines. Take for example the strides and discoveries that have been made in stem cell research. These achievements can serve mankind well and can, perhaps, provide cures for a lot of major diseases. However, the harvesting of stem cells remains a controversial issue. There are many ways in collecting various forms of stem cells, some from unborn fetuses, others from the umbilical cords of infants, retrieving cells from already born fetuses, some from adults. Many are against stem cell research stating it is not God's will that an unborn child be sacrificed this purpose -- nor should a child be aborted before birth. I believe that all life is precious. But if there is a medical reason where an abortion is necessary to save the life of the mother, or if the probability of the infant being able to survive life after birth is very grim, then these steps should be a medical consideration after all alternatives have been ruled out.

Where God has given certain people the gift of preaching, music, art, and other talents, He has bestowed upon others the gifts of healing. This includes giving doctors and research scientists the blueprints for what makes a human function. Like mechanics of automobiles, doctors are "mechanics of humans." Research scientists are the "engineers." To deny them the freedom of carrying out their art and technique just because of religious beliefs and values is wrong. This is preventing God from doing His will for caring and healing for people through the hands of doctors, nurses, and medical technicians.

Stem cell research may very well be an answer provided and inspired by God. But religious beliefs might standing in the way of a major break-through in medicine all because man refuses to open his eyes to the possibility that God could very well be working through research scientists and medical professionals to provide us cures to various diseases. To man: take off your blinders! Open your eyes!

In regards to medicine, governments have the inherent responsibility to ensure that all its citizens remain healthy. An ailing nation affects the economy as well as the overall productivity of the country. Some, however, think that health care should only be available only to those who are able to pay for medical attention. Others say that medical care should only be provided to only those who reside in their countries legally. I say, health care and benefits should be provided to every human being regardless of their national origin or residence, socio-economic status or sexual identity. Diseases know no boundaries. They strike regardless of the origin or type of person or the labels that man has given an individual. Governments have a responsibility of keeping mankind healthy in the world without regard to profits for special interests, insurance companies, ability to pay or not. Access to all medical care, including health maintenance, doctor's visits, and major surgeries, should be provided free of charge without the stress of who or how it is going to be paid for. If this is such a burden on individuals, then again I say, get rid of money. The important matter is to save and maintain life over putting profits into a few individuals. If people are so concerned about reducing medical costs, eliminate insurance companies. These entities only add additional layers of administrative costs and often interfere with medical procedures by dictating advice from non-medical professionals – business people who don't have a medical degree and are not licensed to practice medicine. Yet, they often deny patients benefits and delay necessary procedures. Some have even died because of prolonged delays created by bureaucratic red tape of insurance companies. Many physicians cannot perform their duties of treating patients properly because treatments are "not covered by certain insurance plans."

Health care is not something that should be "rationed" or "managed" by people who are not medically qualified. This includes business people who only possess a business degree – sometimes, not even that. Medicine is the art of saving lives and caring for people. It is a gift given by God to care for his own creation – not something to be "boxed in" or "packaged" like a "profitable commodity." God did not intend for man to make a profit off of human life. Human life was meant to be lived freely and abundantly.

The Internet has done wonders for the world by bridging mankind together. It has provided an excellent way through Facebook, Twitter, and MySpace for people of nations to connect with other peoples in real time. Communication satellites have enabled people to talk over the telephone in different countries. The capability to chat online has enable people to communicate in different time zones where it used to take the dependence of postcards and the local postal service and required days and months to deliver the message. The world is much closer.

But governments have been known for disrupting lines of communications. Such as during demonstrations in the Middle East, governments were known to shut down Internet communications so news would not leak out of their countries. Other efforts are known to attempt to gain more control over the "freedom of communication." In the United States, corporations have been exerting mounting pressure on government agencies for more control over the Internet. Remember that corporations have never been fans of the First Amendment guaranteeing its citizens the freedom of speech and expression. Social networking engines like Facebook, Twitter, Blogger and WordPress only offer a mechanism for real news, un-filtered and uncontrolled by corporate "censorship," and can provide an open channel for whistle blowing. Government and corporations will do anything and everything in their power to shut these mechanisms down. They may serve mankind well, but if it does not serve government or corporations, it is "not good" for the country. In other words, rather than humanity determining what is good for itself, an elite group of people are determining and controlling man's needs and destiny.

Mankind needs the freedom to explore, experiment, create, and invent new things, develop ideas unencumbered by the influences and dictates of business leaders, politicians, and religion – particularly by those who are not qualified to be practicing science, technology and medicine. To prohibit the progress of science and technology is to throw road blocks against the inspiration and will of God.

CHAPTER 22
EDUCATION

Throughout the world, there has been a disparity in the quality of educational levels, differences of scholastic philosophies and methodologies. Even within individual nations, there are disparities of educational levels in metropolitan centers, suburbs, rural areas, social-economic classes and so on. As a result, some people are better educated than others. The world must close the gap in these discrepancies.

The quality of education throughout the entire world should be of a unified, high quality standard that can be offered throughout all socio-economic levels of society, not just to the affluent or to certain races or nationalities but also equally to both sexes, male and female. Educational systems have mirrored the mentality of global corporations – adapting an "assembly line" mentality. Students are not educated for critical thinking, but are prepared on the major goal of "passing standardized tests" not based on individual achievement but almost as if they were being processed, through a system of "quality control."

Such disparities lead to social issues when people are poorly educated and uninformed. In some societies, many students are not really educated – they are just processed along an "educational assembly line." The final result is that individuals really do not know anything when they graduate. They lack the basics of reading, writing, cannot identify exactly where they live on a map nor locate where their own country is located on a globe. In many instances, these individuals cannot properly cite facts in their own country's history, let alone identify famous historical personages.

In some schools, cursive writing is not taught because the trend is for "text messaging." What a lack of foresight. When technology fails, the only way for people to communicate is through such means as cursive writing. Yet some schools do not teach their young students how to write the letters of the alphabet – an essential basic course of study. Learning technology tools should be taught in more advance levels of study, not at basic elementary levels.

The world is failing our children. People and governments are more concerned about the economic stability of their countries and making a profit for corporations rather than considering in the future by investing more in education at all levels: elementary, intermediate, high school, college and university. This is applicable to both public and private institutions. Trends in governments are to curtail funding for education. Government leaders claim they are supportive of education each time they run office, yet do exactly the opposite when they are elected into their positions. Programs in educational institutions like colleges and universities are often reduced while fees are increased. This makes it very unaffordable for many students – especially those in colleges and universities. Students graduate from college and universities heavily in debt due to high tuition and the cost of student loans.

The future of humanity depends on the quality and the development of our children. Nations have become too complacent about making, finding or saving money rather than developing minds, talent, and the sustainability of mankind. The world needs to reverse this trend. Money serves a few people, but it does not serve humanity well. The only way to solve the problems of plaguing mankind is to start eradicating the causes at their very roots. I have been said this before – eliminate money altogether. Adapt another system or means of exchanging goods without the need for currencies and level the system for all nations.

What also complicate things in educational systems in the world are differences in measurement systems. Some nations are stubborn in refusing to adapt a unified form of weights and measures. While most of the world is on the metric system, some countries refuse to adapt to that form of measurement and remain on an Imperial or U.S. customary units. The world needs to simplify the system of weights and measures and adapt to one system. This will help matters in education throughout the entire world where every school teaches a uniform method of weights and measures. When people travel abroad, measuring distances between destinations would be uniform and simplify matters. People would not have to calculate different forms of. Mistakes and errors would be greatly reduced when visiting a foreign country – because every nation has will have adopted the same standards.

Take electricity for example. Much of the world is on 220 volts except for the United States which is still on 110 volts. It would make it much easier for travelers to take appliances using the same voltage without the need for adapters. People would not have to be educated that some countries use one standard of voltage while other countries use another.

Look at the way different countries drive on streets. Some countries drive on the left side of the street while others drive on the right.

We have a very complex world. Nothing is the same, certainly nothing is equal. Equality must also be a part of the educational process. This principle must be taught in early childhood – and an age early enough when the child is capable of understanding the concept throughout the entire world. But it should not only be taught in schools, it must also be taught in the family also.

Education therefore should involve not only teachers in schools, but must involve the parents as well as the grandparents. In contemporary times, schools have been used as a sophisticated child-care facility. That is, the students were dropped off at schools while the parents went to work. Typically, the parents had no role in the child's education. Many times, the grandparents also did not play an active role in the child's early educational process as well.

An African proverb states: "It takes a village to raise a child." This is very true. And the village starts in the home with the immediate family. The parents must be responsible for child's behavioral development. This also includes monitoring the child's behavior both in and out of the house and his or her interactions with other children. Is the child overly aggressive with other children, so as to cause emotional harm such as in the form of bullying? The parents should be held accountable for their children's behavior and discipline. Absentee parenting should no longer be tolerated.

Grandparents should also have an active role in educating the child. Senior citizens normally led inactive lives in retirement. Elderly people can be very useful in the educational process. Besides providing disciplinary support for the parents, the grandparents can play an instrumental role in guiding the child in reading, writing, and basic educational skills. More importantly, serving as mentors and passing along life-long wisdom and family values to the child can be very important.

In contemporary times, parents have relied on other people to be primarily responsible for the education of the child. They have also relied on educational systems to discipline their children as well – a responsibility of the parents and family members. In the future, we must return to the basics where parents and grandparents play an interactive role in educational process as well. Parents must be accountable for the successful development of their children through more involvement and participation in the educational process. However, each student should have the freedom, flexibility, and the environment to learn as an individual without the presence and micro-management of a "helicopter parent."

Also, in modern times, the cutback of funding for schools has resulted in the elimination of arts programming in many school systems. This is wrong and can have long term consequences to the general cultural life of society. It is good to educate students on basic subjects of math, science, and literature. Every child needs a standard level of basic education. But the development of a child demands a well-rounded education. Physical education is not the only component that is important to developing a balanced individual. Arts education, whether it be in fine arts, music, dance, or choral arts, is also necessary to develop a well-rounded individual. To deprive a child of these educational opportunities, is to deprive an individual exposure to a rich cultural life that will benefit them later on in life. Arts of all forms are gifts from God. To deprive young students of opportunities to learn these subjects is to deprive society and humanity of future artists and musicians. The cultural life of the world would die. Also, we must remember that the child-self of each student at this level is still alive and thriving. Many school systems are attempting to destroy that pillar of an individual's development.

Furthermore, by teaching children just the basics is like developing clones. They'll know nothing else and will be incapable of doing anything else. Education, therefore, should be based on cognitive preferences. A core curriculum should be followed from elementary through intermediate. But when children reach high school levels, programs should be tailored to prepare each individual to their individual preferences and strengths. Not a prescribed course of study based on standardized tests developed by psychologists. Many students' cognitive preferences are not compatible with standardized or prescribed coursework. Programs need to be customized for each individual based on personal strengths and potential achievements. The customized course in high school will better prepare the student for advance studies in colleges and universities.

In many societies, preparatory work for college and universities start too late -- typically in high schools. The motivational process and preparation needs to be done at an earlier stage. This is where it takes a village to raise a child. Each child should be guided with encouragement and motivation – not forced, but inspired. The only way to do this is to educate parents and grandparents, and elevate the quality of education throughout the entire world. The educational process should be a fun, motivational endeavor. Not a process of tedious work and overtly concentrated study. The objective is to learn, not cram knowledge. And the learning should be a life-long process of exploration. Education should be an ongoing process. That is how humanity evolves to higher levels of thinking.

Furthermore, rather than being in the forefront of new learning, educational systems have been lagging behind technology. Technology has introduced new ways of learning in the classrooms, but by and large, subjects are taught through traditional methods – especially in colleges and universities. Of course, new technologies such as computers are used more frequently in classrooms, but they are not fully used to their maximum potentials.

Education in the future will not only require a broader course of study, but it also needs to include increased technology in it as well. This applies to all countries. Educational systems lagging behind without technology in their classrooms will be left dramatically behind. The challenge is to raise every nation's educational systems equally. Careers of tomorrow will demand new skills and knowledge. Educational institutions must be keenly aware of these trends and be able to adapt and provide the coursework necessary to meet these demands.

Another way many countries are failing to educate their students are is the area of proper nutrition. Obesity is an epidemic in many countries. Many educational systems have caved into the influences of fast food industries including food processors and restaurants. Rather than eating a proper meal at home, people dine at more fast food eateries now, more than ever before. Much of this can be blamed on corporate life-styles. Work influences have not allowed time for quality family time that once used to be precious in familial life. More adults are forced to work longer hours because of reduced workforces and have less time for their children. For instance, more time at work means less time for the parents to spend helping kids with their homework. This also means not having enough time to prepare a properly, balanced, nutritious meal for growing students. As a consequence, children are fed more "junk" or "processed food" in their daily diet than before. Restaurant chains will claim that what they are serving is not "junk." But when one actually examines the processing of the food, a lot of chemicals and additives are added to the products that are served. Much of the food is not even "natural" but synthetic or fabricated by other chemicals or resources to imitate the "original" food product. Take the popular McDonalds Chicken McNugget. About 40 to 50 percent of a nugget is meat. The other half contain: modified cornstarch, mono-, tri-, and diglycerides, dextrose; lecithin, chicken broth yellow corn flour and more modified cornstarch (for the batter), cornstarch (a filler), vegetable shortening, partially hydrogenated corn oil, citric acid as a preservative, some wheat in the batter, hydrogenated oil could come from soybeans, canola, or cotton rather than corn, depending on the market price and availability:

McNuggets also contain several completely synthetic ingredients, quasiedible substances that ultimately come not from a corn or soybean field but form a petroleum refinery or chemical plant. These chemicals are what make modern processed food possible, by keeping the organic materials in them from going bad or looking strange after months in the freezer or on the road. Such as leavening agents: sodium aluminum phosphate, monocalcium phosphate, sodium acid pyrophosphate, and calcium lactate. These are antioxidants added to keep the various animal and vegetable fats involved in a nugget from turning rancid. Then there are "anti-foaming agents" like dimethylpolysiloxene, added to the cooking oil to keep the starches from binding to air molecules, so as to produce foam during the fry. The problem is evidently grave enough to warrant adding a toxic chemical to the food: Dimethylpolysiloxene is a suspected carcinogen and an established mutagen, tumorigen, and reproductive effector; it's also flammable

But perhaps the most alarming ingredient in a Chicken Mcnugget is tertiary butylhydroquinone, or TBHQ, an antioxidant derived from petroleum that is either sprayed directly on the nugget or the inside of the box it comes in to "help preserve freshness." According to A Consumer's Dictionary of Food Additives, TBHQ is a form of butane (i.e. lighter fluid) the FDA allows processors to use sparingly in our food: It can comprise no more than 0.02 percent of the oil in a nugget. Which is probably just as well, considering that ingesting a single gram of TBHQ can cause "nausea, vomiting, ringing in the ears, delirium, a sense of suffocation, and collapse." Ingesting five grams of TBHQ can kill."[xxiv]

Yet, these are done in order to maximize profits and to keep "costs down." Essentially what is happening is that educational systems, by saving money, and by governments creating "minimum standards" are literally killing the students. Ask the teachers and they will tell you that student performances after noontime meals are very poor -- a lot of students are lethargic. In many poorer districts, students do not even receive breakfast before the beginning of school – not even at home.

The federal government in the United States is making an attempt to provide some assistance to low-income schools and qualifying nonprofit educational institutions by providing free milk, breakfast, and balanced lunch programs. The program is in 72,000 schools across the nation.[xxv] But really, this only covers the tip of the iceberg. So many students are exposed to poor nutrition causing an epidemic of obesity in all states. This is a "village" problem that needs to be addressed by the people.

Corporations and companies everywhere can help by providing their employees a "living wage" rather than a "minimum wage" so that their workers can afford to provide better meals for their families in their homes rather than having to resort to fast-food providers on practically a daily basis. Instead, employers are reluctant to provide their employees a living wage because of costs – especially in fast food restaurants. Many of their employees are forced to work multiple jobs in order to make ends meet. This takes away precious quality time from the family and responsibilities that should be given towards raising their children. This trend also contributes to the high cost of health care in many countries due to illness and obesity related issues and absenteeism from schools.

Many students do not even have a basic knowledge of where food comes from or how to properly identify food or vegetables themselves. In other words, they do not have an idea of what they are even eating. This is highly concerning and the survival of mankind depends on passing along this basic knowledge successfully from generation to generation. Yet, this is not taught as a basic subject in schools.

The education of proper nutrition and diet not only begins in the schools, but it also begins in the home and in the community. Educational systems not only have the responsibility of teaching proper diet and nutrition to its students, but also must lead by example to members of the community through outreach programs. Of course, people will say there is no money for this. Yes there is! Quit spending money on war and weapons, and invest in the money on developing and educating people and students instead! Food manufacturers must take the responsibility of producing and providing healthier products on the markets and eliminating the "junk" it delivers to the stores. After all, why are there so many chemicals and additives of all the products delivered to the stores? Are they really necessary? Are they also driving up the costs? Can they really be avoided? Why not translate the chemical names into layman's words? Food producers must find a better, more efficient way of delivering better quality and healthier food to the market and to schools in order to promote better nutrition and diet. Furthermore, restaurants will also have to change their ways of business to also feature healthier items on their menus. This includes regular restaurants as well as "fast-food" vendors.

Like the proverb says, "It takes a village to raise a student." The world must do all it can to eliminate obesity by eradicating the causes creating this epidemic in the world.

CHAPTER 23
SOCIAL ISSUES

The world has many social issues to contend with -- many of which keep mankind from moving forth in the right direction. They are often matters which weigh our thoughts and concerns down and take our focus off of realizing our dreams and goals for a better life.

ADDICTION, DRUGS AND ALCOHOL

The world has a very peculiar way of dealing with drug addiction, illegal drugs, and alcohol consumption. When misused, they are all harmful to the body. It would be wise not to consume them at all. In some parts of the world, what are considered as "illegal drugs" are perfectly acceptable and consumed in other parts of the world.

The weakness of man has tempted him to use these substances. Throughout history, he has continuously sought ways to put his mind into another realm. The danger of this is that many do not think or act rationally. Their behavioral patterns are such that they are heavily impaired by these substances. Seeking to create a better world for mankind demands a clear consciousness – pure thinking. Some drugs relaxes the body and mind into doing this – especially if the body is heavily stressed by other external influences. The best way to reduce drug addiction is to seek ways to improve our environment. Seek ways of reducing our daily stress and causes for the need to seek out substances that would alter our minds. Help these people seek a better world by improving the setting that they live in. If you are creating a stressful environment, reduce the stressful factors in your situation. Workplaces and the stresses they create are notorious for creating an unhealthful environment which often leads to uncontrolled hypertension, anxiety, depression, and other behavioral problems. Many of these factors can also lead to the need for psychiatric help, therefore driving up the cost of medical care not only in the family, but also the workplace.

Family life can also cause stressful conditions upon an individual. Family members should seek counseling to reduce the stress factors in their daily living and reduce the circumstances in their households that can lead to drug abuse (i.e. eliminate the presence of narcotics and alcohol).

As for alcoholic beverages, I have to admit, I was a budding alcoholic. A couple times becoming seriously ill from alcoholic poisoning taught me a valuable life-long lesson. It is something that should be respected and not abused. The creation of beer, wine, and liquor is an art form. Like all other art forms, it is something to be appreciated. Some alcoholic beverages contain antioxidants which are beneficial for the human body and are good when taken in moderation. These beverages have different effects on each individual. Some tolerate alcohol better than others. One should appreciate the beverage as a product of art, but not abuse it by over indulging. Like all other mind altering substances, use it responsibly. Don't drink until you become so drunk, that you cannot think clearly, walk straight, or lose consciousness. If inebriated, you cannot help move mankind in the right direction.

One final thought on alcohol consumption. There is a Muslim practice I highly respect and appreciate. It is a valuable lesson for the entire world. That is the *total* abstinence of alcoholic beverages. One has to remember that alcoholic beverages in modern times are far more potent than in Biblical times. Then, you would have to be drinking all day in order to get drunk. In contemporary times, all it would take is as much as one sip to some people, one glass or bottle to others. Therefore, it would be wiser not to consume it at all.

DISASTERS

In Biblical times, disasters were once thought to have been caused by God --that they were a punishment to man for his deeds or misdeeds. This was totally false and modern evidence and facts only prove that we live on an imperfect planet full of "faults." The tectonic plates on Earth are in constant motion which causes unpredictable earthquakes. Depending on the location of the quakes and their magnitude, they can be quite disastrous and devastating. Cities that were built near coastlines especially suffered major damages such as Sendai, Japan in March 2011 and Haiti in 2010. Religious believers say these are signs of the "end time." These episodes are really just random unfortunate events on Earth's history. The time to really be concerned about the end of the planet is when major earthquakes, dormant volcanoes erupt, and motion happens continuously throughout the day and night on both sides of the ocean. That would be a time to be concerned. But as for now, there is no need for panic and fear.

When disasters occur, they often reveal how little prepared mankind is for such events. In Japan, for example, nuclear power plants were built to withstand an earthquake of about 7.0 magnitude. However, when the trembler of 2011 occurred, the magnitude of that quake was 8.9 – over a thousand times greater than the power plant was designed to withstand. As a result, major damages were seen around the world resulting in tsunamis and heavily damaged a nuclear generating station at Fukushima. As I mentioned before, consumers still see the after effects of this disaster though the radioactivity of fishes in parts of the world -- mainly the west coast of the United States and Canada.

When Hurricane Katrina struck New Orleans, the city was unprepared for such devastation. To make matters even worse, aid to the victims was slow to come. Many people had lost their lives in the aftermath because they could not get help in a timely manner. Governmental agencies were unprepared for such a disaster. Much of the assistance was disorganized.

But the interesting matter about the aid to Katrina victims -- most of the people were minority, elderly, and many lived in poverty. Is this why aid to this city was so slow to come? Often, aid to foreign nations seemed to be quicker than the response to New Orleans. Was this an actual demonstration of people being treated as second class citizens during a time of disaster? Aide during and after a major disaster should be provided equally regardless of an area's socio-economic status or its people. To treat people differently in times of disasters is wrong and should not be tolerated.

In the past, people have been more concerned about the costs of rebuilding civilizations rather than coming to the aid of humanity and assisting their fellow man. Human beings have become secondary to the importance of materialism. In the new world, the focus will always be on mankind. Man will eventually find a way of eliminating the importance of cost of rebuilding cities and eventually, money will no longer become a factor or burden on rebuilding after a disaster. The example of New Orleans was only an example of man's concern for profit and materialism over the importance of aiding his fellow men in distress. Would he act differently if the disaster fell upon New York City, Chicago, San Francisco, or Los Angeles if the devastation was equal to or greater than the disaster in Sendai, Japan?

POVERTY, HOMELESSNESS, AND WORLD HUNGER

Man was never known to share his wealth equally. There have been countless illustrations of this over time and history. Kings and queens kept reaping the bulk of the harvests of their subjects while the people were given only a paltry share of their efforts. In the corporate world, the problem has been even magnified.

As the saying goes, "A penny for you, a dollar for me." Some reap the profits while many others are forced to live disadvantaged lives in poverty, homelessness, and starvation. Some people say, this is a "choice." The "choice" has been dictated for them by a few people of this Earth who profit and cause a great imbalance of life on this planet.

Some have lost their lives prematurely because of the behaviors of those who created these conditions. There is an example in California where a civic government employee took his life by jumping off a roof after learning that his job was going to be outsourced to a private company.[xxvi]

Society has not learned how to offer benevolent assistance to those being terminated by offering them replacement services and retraining or alternatives for earning an income. Their attitude is generally very greedy and selfish in itself. They care less about the welfare of their fellow man, but care more for the financial bottom line. This causes great hardship and disparity on the people in their communities. But it is no concern for them for they think they are "safe." – at least for now. People have placed themselves on an illusionary "totem pole." They think the higher in stature they are on the pole, the safer they are from the worries of society. Disasters affect all of mankind, regardless of economic status. What one has materially right now, can be easily taken away and destroyed in less than five seconds by God.

Then, when one is laid off and unable to pay the bills, society is often unforgiving of the individual and often places blame on the person for losing his or her job, unable to earn an income. This affects the individual's ability to pay the bills in a timely manner. As a result, these long-term unemployed are unable to return to work, suffer from to a poor credit ratings, and are generally considered outcasts of society -- all because of their inability to make money.

The social issue *is* money. Although it has benefitted some people on Earth, it has displaced many people out of their homes, caused tremendous financial difficulties, of and broken families, starvation, and world hunger.

Influential people with tremendous wealth wield their powers in government to prohibit crops that can be produced on farms. Potential cash crops (i.e., industrial hemp) that can actually benefit mankind, but are labeled with false facts and information and passed on to consumers that they are something "bad" for the people. Generally, the information is full of lies and fabricated, misleading information. Again, an act of helping a few people increase their profits rather than acting towards benefitting humanity as a whole – such as eliminating world hunger.

GAYS, LESBIANS, BISEXUALS, TRANSGENDERS -- SEXUAL IDENTITY

Homosexuality existed since early man and is nothing new. Man has always had a problem with homosexuality. Around the 10th Millenium BC, about the end of the Paleolithic Era, mankind made artifacts which suggested an appreciation of homosexual eroticism through such examples as graffiti in caves, buildings and phallic statues.

Notable examples of homosexuality were found in nobility and government leaders of the times, notably in Egypt and Crete.

It was an acceptable form of sexual identity until around 149 BC, when the Lex Scantinia, a Roman law, regulated homosexuality for the first time on record. This was an ancient law that penalized a sex crime against a free born minor. The law may also have been used to prosecute adult male citizens who willingly took a passive role in having sex with other men. It was thus aimed at protecting the citizen's body from sexual abuse, but did not prohibit homosexual behavior as such, as long as the passive partner was not a citizen in good standing.[xxvii]

In the 1st Century BC, there were the first instances of same-sex marriage during the reign of Augustus in Rome (42 BC – 39 BC). Around 26 BC – 18 BC, Romans and Greeks tolerated love and sex among men. Two Roman Emperors publicly married men, some had gay lovers themselves, Nero and Elagabalus, and homosexual prostitution was taxed. However, like the Greeks, passivity and effeminacy were not tolerated, and an adult male freeborn Roman could lose his citizen status if willingly taking.

In the 4th Century, religion began to exert its influence on homosexuality. Around 305-306, the Council of Elvira, now Granada, Spain, was representative of the Western European Church and it barred pederasts the right to Communion.[xxviii]

In 314, the Council of Ancyra (now Ankara, Turkey) and the Eastern European Church representative excluded sacraments for 15 years to unmarried men under the age of 20 who were caught in homosexual acts and excluded the man for life if he was married and over the age of 50.[xxix]

In 342, the first law was issued in the Theodosian Code against same-sex marriage came under the rule of Christian emperors, Constantius II and Constans. In the year 390, Christian emperors Valentinian II, Theodosius I and Carcadius declared homosexual sex life to be illegal and those who were guilty of it were condemned to be burned alive in public. Between 390-405 AD, Nonnus of Panopolis wrote the *Dionysiaca,* the last known piece of literature for nearly 1,000 years to celebrate homosexual passion.

Since that time, homosexuals have been scapegoats for practically every travesty on Earth including earthquakes. For centuries following, homosexuality was a major crime punishable by death. In more modern times, trends have begun to reverse the highly illogical argument against homosexuality.

In 1920, the word "Gay" is used for the first time in reference to homosexuality. Following that year in England, an attempt to make lesbianism illegal for the first time in Britain's history failed. In 1922, a new criminal code comes into force in the USSR officially decriminalizing homosexual acts. In 1933, a new Danish law decriminalizes homosexuality as did Uruguay in 1934.

In 1940, Iceland decriminalized homosexuality as did Switzerland in 1942, and Sweden in 1944. During this period, however, gays and lesbians were still not off the hook. During the Third Reich (World War II), they were sent to concentration camps in Europe and made to wear a pink triangle patch on their clothing.

In 1988, Sweden became the first country to pass laws protecting homosexuals regarding social services, taxes, and inheritances. Belize and Israel decriminalized sodomy and other sexual acts between men. The European Court struck down the Irish law criminalizing male-to-male sex on the grounds of privacy.

In 1989, Western Australia decriminalizes homosexuality while Liechtenstein legalizes homosexuality. Demark is the first country in the world to enact registered partnership laws (like a civil union) for same-sex couples, with most of the same rights as marriage, excluding the right to adoption, until June 1010 and the right to marriage in a church.

Regardless of these trials and tribulations, there have been countless of occasions were LGBT's have served their countries honorably in times of war and disasters. Many have volunteered and sacrificed their lives so that others may enjoy the freedoms that they enjoy. However, societies have treated them very harshly in return for their service. They have denied them equal opportunities and privileges typically to ordinary couples. Many cultures have a very bad habit of doing this. That is, they appreciate their service, but are never truly thankful to them as fellow human beings, just because they belong to another "class of people." It can be in the form of different sexual identity, race, color, ethnicity, or religious belief. As long as they are serving in a military force, they are considered as "X." But when they leave the unit, they are classified as everything else (i.e. "A,B,C,Y,Z, etc.). They are never considered or treated as equals, as common humans. Therefore, they are not entitled to the same rights and privileges that they personally fought for while in the service. Humans need to learn how to be grateful for everything in life. This includes the sacrifices that were made not only by minorities, but also from gays, lesbians, bisexuals, and transgenders. The practice of racism and discrimination must cease, for some of the behavioral actions of a few may cause the untimely, premature death of another person or the brutal beating of another.

In contemporary times, young people have difficulties trying to adjust and cope with peer pressure. Bullying of gays, for example, is something that cannot be ignored, but happens in daily life – especially during school years. Some individuals are taunted and harassed because of their sexual identities. This is wrong. Not only should the misbehaving child/teenager should be held accountable for their actions, but also their parents. Much of this is dictated by internal family values, religious beliefs, and intolerance. These need to change quickly as man moves on. It is an educational process that affects not only students, but adults as well. Lives need to be saved, not tragically lost, because of unbearable pressures on individuals, and the lack of support from their parents.

Many uneducated people taunt gays as being ignorant and "uneducated." This is totally false and incorrect. The people expressing these slurs and lies are the ones that need to be educated. Many base their arguments on Bible theory. If the Bible claims that homosexuality is evil, then they assume this to be so without any foundation for the truth. Since the Bible was written, God has revealed the truth behind homosexuality through medicine. Homosexuality is not a matter of choice as many are led to believe.[xxx] It's all genetic. It's a matter of the DNA in each individual.

"Special form of natural selection based on an organism's ability to mate. Some animals possess characteristics that are more attractive to potential mates, such as the distinctive plumage of some male birds. Individuals with such characteristics mate at higher rates than those without, ensuring more next generation offspring will inherit the desirable trait. As generations procreate the desirable trait becomes increasingly common, further boosting the sexual disadvantage for individuals who lack the desired trait. The effect can be particularly dramatic when one individual controls mating with a large number of potential partners."[xxxi]

Mankind must develop a tolerance for all of humanity and allow individuals to develop their own personal sexual identities – not dictated by peer pressure, religion, or familial values or traditions. As I have said before, this matter is genetically influenced and engrained in each individual. It cannot be changed by external influences. Man must learn how to accept scientific evidence and learn how to love each individual for who they are, not what society expects them to be. Give each individual the room and freedom to accelerate on his or her own. Provide loving care, guidance, and interaction, not dictates or imposing your own personal expectations on them. Do not hover over your child around the clock like the proverbial 'helicopter parent." And worst of all – going to the opposite extreme -- avoid taking an active part in your child's life at all.

Parents, do not be dismayed or discouraged that your

child is a homosexual. There is nothing you can do, nor is it your fault that he or she resulted as such. It is not a punishment on you or the child. It is just a natural process that can happen to virtually anyone. Parents of homosexual children often punish themselves for what they have done. Many "disown" their children by, for example, kicking the child out of their homes and dwellings. Japanese families are notorious for doing this for they think these children have been "cursed." In other countries, homosexuals are killed because of their sexual identity. The entire world needs to be educated on the facts of homosexuality and not take adverse actions against it just because their religions indicate something to the contrary. The world must mature its behavior and thinking to accept all humans as equals. Presently, the world still behaves and thinks in the dark ages. Everyone needs to come into the light of modern truth based on factual evidence, not theoretical suppositions.

What has been thought of homosexuality throughout the ages is entirely myth and fable. Many of these myths have led to the unfortunate deaths of countless many innocent humans, all because they have been wrongly judged without factual or scientific evidence. Now that this evidence exists, there is absolutely nothing to be ashamed of. God loves and cares for every human being. This includes LGBT's. No if's, and's, or but's, or this said that, and that said this. What has been said or written before is what *man* has said or written – not by any celestial entity.

RACISM AND DISCRIMINATION

We already have a problem with borders that separate us from coming closer together as a world community. But besides these, people have created artificial barriers that separate them which are racial. Throughout time, people have permitted the color of one's skin to separate them, causing fear, mistrust, and misunderstandings, and resentment commonly known as racial divides. Minorities not only exist in the United States, but also in other countries in the Middle East, Europe, and Asia. Discrimination and racism is prevalent throughout the entire world.

Throughout history, there have been numerous cases where one race has placed themselves higher than another. Some have enslaved other races. Yet others, thinking that they are more superior than other groups of human beings, treat rivals harshly and severely. Some races in certain countries are considered as outcasts. Mankind has always had difficulties coming to understand that *it is one race* – the human race. In modern times, significant strides have been made to bridge the gap in race relations. But there is still a lot of work to be done. Recent genetic studies indicate that everyone has come from one race of people in Africa. We all share the same heritage – the same Adam(s). Whether we have been created or evolved from other life forms is unimportant. The pertinent matter is not to look back to the point where it causes so much distress and argument, but to look forward, build relationships, and redirect a ship that has gone astray because of our differences and misunderstandings.

Tolerance or intolerance begins in the home and at a very early age. Parents and grandparents must educate their children and grandchildren as to the importance and values of tolerance and accepting people of other races and cultures. But what is fed into the households via radio and television newscasts is equally important. Editorial departments of journalistic resources have a responsibility of balanced reporting.

All too frequently, "news" on radio and television is that of the negative kind --especially if it concerns groups of people or those of different religions. People already have a bad habit of stereotyping other groups of ethnicities. Individuals who fall into one group are often associated with behaviors that are "common" to that group of people. The individual him or herself is never appreciated nor respected as a separate, unique human being -- but always associated with a certain class or group. By frequently broadcasting and televising images of people which are negative and violent, this gives others the false impression that they (the other group of people) always behave like that. Therefore, false perspectives and impressions are created. This is particularly worrisome when people who have watched these news events have never travelled out of their domain to learn about nor meet with people in foreign countries or cultures. In the United States only about 39% of the population have passports.[xxxii] They have always led a secluded lifestyle but have always obtained their "facts" from news outlets.

News bureaus can be influential in changing these perspectives by broadcasting and televising the positive aspects of people and their accomplishments as well. But in modern times, everything is skewed towards the negative aspects of human behavior. If you continuously focus on violence and negative behavior in the world, it will continue to manifest itself. The more often negative news and events are shown on television, the more people tend to be critical and voice negativity. There is less appreciation for life in the world.

Humanity needs to change its perspective and appreciate life by recognizing the positive aspects of living rather than being constantly critical. More and more, people tend to overly criticize and never recognize the positive. Look for example, of reality game shows and the feedback given by judges. Take a pen and paper and jot down the negative comments versus the positive comments that are offered to a contestant. Typically, you would see that the negatives outweigh the positives. The world needs to be more positive and less critical.

If we want peace and to eliminate racism and discrimination, then we must let peace manifest itself into reality. We can do a lot of this by de-emphasizing the negative things we do and say both in the home and over the airwaves. Dramatization over the airwaves is no excuse for "just because it sells." Media has a responsibility of correcting bad behavior in society. And, it can use its influences to do so by changing the stories it broadcasts on television and in the theatres.

FREEDOM

Many things have been said about freedom by many famous and not so notable people. My wish for freedom to the people of the world comes from the words of Simone de Beauvior:

"I wish that every human life might be pure transparent freedom."

But many truths have also been said about freedom that we all need to be concerned about. As an unknown author once said:

"No one is free when others are oppressed."

How strikingly true and accurate these few words are in today's world. No one is free when we still have others in the world are oppressed, living in poverty, starvation, homelessness, and treated with inequality. Mankind still has a lot of work on its plate, *before we can even imagine to move in the right direction.* For ages, men have conditioned themselves to be ruled by a minority whom they've empowered to serve in authoritarian roles. The problem is, these people have neglected the fact that they were called *to serve, not to be served.* The problem is, power has quickly gone to their heads; freedom and liberty were taken away; people were enslaved to their rulers as these people placed themselves on pedestals. These are all illusions that people have the power to overcome. The populace still has the power to make changes in the world by and reclaiming the liberties and freedoms granted to men by God. The people should not be intimidated by a ruling few, but it should be otherwise reversed. The irresponsible few should be intimidated by the majority of the people they serve, for in a true world of freedom and liberty, the powers rest with the people – not with a few appointed or elected government leaders or corporate executives.

As long as oppression of the people exists in any form, whether it be by governmental rule or corporate management, there will never be freedom. The power to reclaim this freedom resides in the people. For mankind to move in the right direction, the citizens must have the courage to take destiny into their own hands from their oppressors.

HUMAN RIGHTS

I've already talked a little about human rights and equality for gays, lesbians, bisexuals, and transgenders. These individuals deserve as much as everyone else in respect to equality, equal rights, privileges, opportunities, benefits, and treatment simply as a fellow human being.

The same applies to women's rights around the world. Women are not treated with equal dignity and respect. In the U.S. business life, women are paid much less than men for equal work. In other countries, women have often been considered as "property" or "inferior humans." Yet, they are expected to do just as much work, if not more, than their male counter parts including giving birth to newborn infants. Women are often abused, beaten and tortured often by irresponsible mates who are influenced by alcohol, drugs, rage, or false information. Yet when their male counterparts commit the same crimes, they are often given lighter sentences.

This imbalance in society must be corrected. The movement of mankind in the right direction involves both mutual male and female interaction, equally as one– one gender not greater than the other. In the new rebirth of the world, women will be treated equally with men – such as equal salaries and benefits. The age of male dominance will come to an end for it will be important for both sexes to survive equally.

In regards to women's rights, reproductive rights should belong freely and rightfully to each female individual, not dictated or legislated by governments unless it is for the protection of these individuals. Each female should have the freedom to decide when reproduction is appropriate or not. Not forced upon unwillingly by men though coercion or violence. The trafficking of women as sex slaves should also not be tolerated in any society. Women should be respected highly as human beings – not as objects for pleasure.

Furthermore, the privacy between two consenting human beings behind closed doors should also be respected. A lot of people have a bad habit of getting involved in other people's affairs – none of it their business. However, they proceed to make it their business anyway by declaring themselves as self-appointed guardians of public morals. This leads to a lot of problems -- political leaders become involved and write unnecessary legislation governing the behavior of consenting adults. Society has gone to the point where it has micromanaged everything -- including people's lives. Certainly, there are some things that should not be tolerated, such as incest and child sexual abuse. But controlling people's lives should not be legislated to the point where it denies equal freedoms and opportunities. Some religious believers overstep their bounds by asserting their values and beliefs on others. This often infringes on the freedom of religion for others since religion is a personal matter. Religion, doctrines or beliefs should never the basis of laws which infringe upon those who believe to the contrary. Laws should only be adopted based on the will of the entire populace – not a simple majority or minority that has the most money and the loudest voice. This is why, in some countries, there is the concept of separation of church and state, also in theocracies as in Iran. But more often than ever, this concept is rapidly being ignored in favor of certain religious groups.

Women should also not bear the total responsibility of housework. In earlier times, the female half of the couple was responsible for raising the children, taking care of needs of the house, doing the chores around the home and doing things that males generally did not do. This needs to change. In the last 50, it has improved in the United States. The tasks and responsibilities of the home should be a shared responsibility. This includes raising the children, infants as well, cooking meals, laundry, and everything else that were once only delegated to women (and least appreciated for).

Women have taken on more responsibilities in society and should be recognized for their accomplishments, especially in terms of compensation. No longer can it be argued that males have a greater responsibility by going off to fight wars. In modern times, women and mothers, sacrifice their lives and time by going to the battlefields also.

There is also a great imbalance of wealth in the world. This imbalance is causing the oppression of people in the world of all forms. In some countries, children are placed in the workforce almost as "slave labor." This "cheap labor" benefits wealthy executives and stockholders in foreign countries while the children are paid pennies for their work, yet forced to labor long hours. Yet, these occupations were once filled by people in other countries who were eventually terminated from their positions for reasons of being "too expensive, high benefits." These people not only lost their jobs, but their homes as well. The time will soon come when corporate executives, too, will be served with "pink slips" and their "services will no longer be needed." It's not to say that they will lose their jobs permanently, it is just that when everyone else receives an equitable salary in the new world, the dynamics of business will dramatically change. Their "bad behavior" will no longer be tolerated.

One closing thought on this section. Where there should be a separation between church and state. The same should apply for business – a separation between corporation and state. For, the state belongs only to the people and by the people.

IMMIGRATION

The New Colossus

Not like the brazen giant of Greek fame,
With conquering limbs astride from land to land;

Here at our sea-washed, sunset gates shall stand
A mighty woman with a torch, whose flame
Is the imprisoned lightning, and her name
Mother of Exiles. From her beacon-hand
Glows world-wide welcome; her mild eyes command
The air-bridged harbor that twin cities frame.
"Keep ancient lands, your storied pomp!" cries she
With silent lips. "Give me your tired, your poor,
Your huddled masses yearning to breathe free,
The wretched refuse of your teeming shore.
Send these, the homeless, tempest-tost to me,
I lift my lamp beside the golden door!"

Emma Lazarus,
July 22, 1849 – November 19, 1887
American Poet

How ironic, that in a country of the United States, such a beautiful poem would stand at the base of the Statue of Liberty while the rest of her people is taking strides to shut out immigration by building walls and fences along the Mexican border; passing legislation to shoot illegal immigrants from helicopters; having police stop every Latino (including American citizens) for being suspected of illegal immigration. A nation which has been famous for welcoming the homeless and oppressed of other countries, would take strides to close its doors to its own neighbors all in the fear of "terrorism."

If a country seeks immigration reform, it should open its doors – not close them. Take Europe for example, countries which have been known in history for fighting wars, created railways which brought them closer together, created a common, unified currency and are not living in so much paranoia as the United States. In fact, speaking about stereotyping people, the country is taking steps to build walls along Mexico to keep illegal immigration out from its southern border. It is not building walls or fences along its Canadian border.

The United States is notorious for creating monsters, dictators, rogue governments and oppressive factions to overthrow undesirable governments that eventually come back to haunt the country. The U.S. should save its money and keep their noses out of other countries' internal affairs.

The United States has also built an empire where other countries are highly envious of their achievements and accomplishments. So much that they have left other nations behind. If the United States wants to fight terrorism, raise the levels of other countries so that every nation is on an equal playing field -- that there would be no cause for envy and jealousy. This is not to say that the U.S. should exert its influence on any given country. The process must be entirely voluntary. Yet on the other hand, poorer countries must not be enslaved to the advancements of richer countries. Rather than exporting military weapons and technology, the United States should export educational technology, agricultural technology, and culture – peaceful products designed to preserve and uplift humanity -- not things that will destroy human life. Only provide military assistance only in case of emergency and disasters – but do not continue to supply nations with armament and weapons.

The United States should follow the European model by opening its doors and build high-speed railways between its neighbors, not close its doors. This is the only path to immigration reform. To note, the United States has still yet to build high-speed, fuel-efficient rail systems within its borders. Rather, it spends its funds heavily on an over-bloated defense budget instead of infrastructure and transportation system improvement.

To fight terrorism effectively, communicate with your enemies directly. Better yet, don't create enemies in the first place --rather, make friends instead.

CHAPTER 24

THE PLANET AND THE ENVIRONMENT

Mother Earth is like fine china: she is very delicate. She provides a lot to those who take care of her. But to those who mismanage her resources, there can be severe consequences.

Man has forgotten that he is made up from elements of Mother Earth. When we pass on, physically we return to Earth. However, elements which make up our individual intelligence, our individual spirit, are acquired from other parts of the universe. The individual spirit that drives our behavior comes from a wide spectrum of resources in the universe. Some people are heavily influenced by civilizations that prevail through war and violence and do not have respect for their own planet. Others originate from peaceful civilizations. These civilizations have a respect for their environment and planets and underscore their connectivity with all of the elements in their environment.

On Earth, there is a mixed bag of influences. That's because some people are driven by war, others are driven by peace. Unfortunately, man has not been a good steward in taking care of his domain. He has continued to pollute the air and waters; continued to produce products that are harmful to the environment (i.e., petroleum, toxic products); continues to manufacture goods inefficiently without regard for the environment; purchasing large trucks, sports utility vehicles SUVs), and vans -- driving large, gas-guzzling vehicles with no passengers. Some countries have yet to educate their people on the practices of conservation which includes driving smaller, fuel efficient vehicles – especially when driving alone. And the pathetic observation about this fact is that this is in an area of the country where mass transportation in the region is practically non-existent (such as Los Angeles County). Where it would be easier to just take these large vehicles off the market and replace them with smaller fuel efficient automobiles, manufacturers insist on the continuance of these large vehicles, disregarding the fact that the world's oil supply is dwindling and prices are rising rapidly. Has anyone there given any thought to what they're doing to Mother Earth?

Man is so concerned about the loans that countries have taken out and how a few countries have already declared bankruptcy (i.e., Greece). They are so focused on the money or financial problems that they have totally ignored the *loan that Mother Earth has given to man*. Man has continuously taken from Mother Earth, but never bothered to replenish her supply. Take crude oil for example. Man is so fixated on crude oil as his primary source of energy, that he has neglected or failed to invest in other forms of energy in a timely manner. As a result, the clock is ticking until the world's oil supply will quickly diminish. After all, only so many dinosaurs sacrificed their lives so that mankind may eventually benefit from their oil.

Of course, politics and special interests had a large part

in slowing down the search for viable solutions. Man has historically had an inherent problem – he acts on things too late. He generally never acts on anything proactively – such as planning ahead and taking action before the problem actually surfaces. He always had the bad habit of procrastinating.

Global warming is another issue that man will act upon when it is too late. Some think global warming is all a hoax. Many scientists say that the ozone is damaged by the things that man has already done and that corrective steps need to be taken now. I am not greatly knowledgeable on the issue, but there are signs on Earth (such as the melting of the polar ice caps and glaciers), that suggest that there is an urgency to the matter.

The general fear by those who say that taking corrective measures are too costly are mainly concerned about their profits – with very little regard for the welfare of mankind or the future. These people are more concerned about the present. The world is concerned about Earth's future and survivability. Yet, where are the government leaders in all this debate? Actually, debating is slowing matters down. If there is something urgent that needs attention, don't depend on your governments to solve it, let alone provide funding for it. If they are not going to fund activities such as Family Planning Centers (Planned Parenthood) and National Public Radio, or programs that are truly in the public's interest, then can you really expect the government to fund an urgency such as global warming? What do you expect from a government that spends more on a corporate war machine designed to kill people, rather than on programs that enhance, save, and benefit human life? Only Heaven knows that there is something drastically wrong with this picture.

Life on Earth was made to be enjoyed in abundance

by every living creature -- not only by human beings, but other life forms and animals as well. Man, has found ways to disrupt that enjoyment by limiting, and in some cases, denying resources to many. He continues to slaughter not only his own species, but other animals as well; overfishing the oceans driving some sea life to near extinction.

He was expected to live harmoniously, in balance with the Earth -- not to destroy it by reckless practices and violent behavior.

Should man continue his bad behavior by not respecting Mother Earth, he will eventually find that the planet will no longer provide for him. He will *default* on his loan with Mother Earth.

If mankind is to move in the right direction, the behavior of man must be corrected. The survival of the planet depends on it.

SECTION FIVE

MOVING MANKIND IN THE RIGHT DIRECTION

CHAPTER 25
SHEDDING OLD VALUES
AND BEHAVIORS

Shedding old values and behaviors is like taking the security blanket away from a child. But time has come to shed the security blanket and grow out of our adolescent, feeble minds and begin to take our place in the universe as a society of higher thinking. If we continue to hold on to old values, then the world will never change or progress. These old habits will continue to manifest themselves in our daily lives. Even if some of us who desire change, those who refuse to change and hang onto their old values will continue hinder those who do, and will prevent progress.

For too long in man's history, we have always depended on some form of currency. It has been like a baby's "milk bottle." We've been sucking on it too long, have become over dependent on money, that so much so man does not know how to live or survive without it. Some have become so dependent on it that they horde money and are driven by insatiable greed and power. They use this power to cheat, influence political leaders and use the money to buy elections in a "democratic" society which otherwise subverts the true definition and spirit of "democracy."

The more money one has, the more power he thinks he can use to control governments. Take the world's bankers for example. Their access to the world's currency has given them the illusional power to influence and control some of the most powerful government leaders in the world – as if these leaders were puppets to a singular banking organization that pulls the strings. If you doubt this, just look at the behaviors of the leaders of your country. Are they really serving in your best interest? Or, are they serving special interests, not the will of the people?

Unfortunately, some political parties are dedicated towards benefitting only the rich and ensure that their political representatives enact legislation that favor the wealthy while taking away benefits and services for the majority of people. When it comes time to adopting a budget for the government, they ensure that the elite rich in their countries are rewarded, while funding is cut for programs and services that benefit the majority of the citizens. Arts, education, medical and social services are programs that are particularly targeted. They take taxpayers' money and give it to the rich, who often don't pay taxes at all, or are provided with lucrative tax loopholes.

There is an imbalance of wealth in the world causing tremendous pain and disparity to millions, let alone forcing people into starvation, homelessness and poverty. The current monetary system is highly inequitable and it would appear that a small number of people would like it this way.

Money has fueled the appetite for greed among many, but not all. That's because there hasn't been enough of it to go around. Like the baby being weaned off the milk bottle, mankind must wean itself off the things which cause so much pain, suffering and inequality in the world. Either find and adopt a more equitable currency system, or simply just rid the world of money all together. The Zeitgeist Movement offers one solution to a money-free world.[xxxiii] There may be more. But nevertheless, money is one value that must be shed.

Another way is to simply and abruptly disregard the value of any currency at all – stop its flow around the world, and quickly adapt to a money-free society by no longer recognizing the worth of currencies. Where men have declared money to be of some value, mankind has the power to also declare it worthless and change to something else. Political power is only an illusion. People have power only if other people give it to them. But, power can be easily taken away if the majority of the people will it so. The will of the people *is* mightier than money -- particularly if money itself is no longer recognized as something of value in society.

There is power in numbers. The people of the world will have and need to take destiny into their own hands by reclaiming the power and control from the few that are out to erode democracy and turn this world into a Plutonian society (a lower world civilization, or an inferno).

Take for example the illegal legislative actions in Wisconsin, Michigan, and Ohio. Government leaders there have denied their people the right to collective bargaining and organizing unions. What has been done in these states is basically the flashpoint of what may trigger larger events in the future. What their legislators did was simply a subversion of democracy and disregard for its laws in order to fulfill a narrow-minded party agenda – not take action for the good of its people or abide by the orders of the courts. Simply said, they put themselves "above the law." Or, in other terms, "to put a blow to the middle class."

Periodically, governments should review themselves

to ensure that they are serving their constituents to the best of their ability *as servants*, not career politicians. Also while doing this review, they should also ensure that they are working efficiently and spending the citizenry's money responsibly and wisely as stewards of the public trust. If a government is spending more on defense expenses, and not more on uplifting its people with human-oriented programs and services, then the citizens should have the right to make radical alterations and wholesale changes to their government. The government, after all, belongs to and serves the people. The people do not serve the government. Of course, perhaps a little tweaking and minor adjustment or change here and there is necessary. Nevertheless, the government and the people should create a non-partisan, unbiased citizens' department of oversight and quality assurance to ensure that the country is receiving what it expects.

All too long, government leaders have viewed themselves as members of a highly exclusive "club." The club is influenced by corporate and special interest money and their legislative behaviors often reflect that they are being influenced by other entities other than their elected constituents. When legislative leaders perceive themselves as members of an exclusive club in a democratic government, it is time for wholesale changes regardless of their political affiliations. Amendments to the Constitution should ensure that there are term limits in all elected offices including justices of the Supreme Court. This is to ensure that no one member of the executive branch, legislature, or justice department considers him or herself as a "career politician."

Political leaders of the future should be totally independent, unbiased, and free from any external influences that may corrupt their judgment while in office. Furthermore, they should be expected to pass qualification exams, written and oral, before an unbiased panel to ensure that they understand the Constitution and to ensure that they understand the oath that they are about to affirm before taking office. It is pathetic that in some countries, government leaders do not even understand or know the constitution of their own country. Just as bad, some demonstrate a very poor basic knowledge of their country's history. Not only should these people be skillful servants of the people, but they should also be expected to be highly educated with a post graduate college degree.

Another behavior that man must correct is its long history of violence. Humans, themselves have a natural "mean streak." This can be controlled. It is often this dark side of man that has caused him to kill, go to war, and fight with other people. He plays violent games (American football, hockey and boxing). Just look at all the video games that are out on the market today that are full of violence. People in some countries have a bad habit of paying a lot of money to see men beat up other men. Of course, this is not new. People have been doing this since the days of the Roman Empire -- an insatiable appetite for violence. This can be curbed and must be corrected by changing our behaviors and raising our levels of thinking.

Violence is characteristic of species of a lower denomination – a lower level of thinking. Societies of higher civilizations do not resort to violence but find alternatives to solving problems and avoiding the manifestation of violence in their daily living and cultures. Why does man have to live with violence? Why can't societies control their behavior if they are civilized, and of intellectual mind?

Then we must ask ourselves, what benefit can we achieve by killing one another? Why do you want to kill or harm me? Why do I want to kill or harm you? What purpose does killing or harming others serve? What will it take to raise our levels of thinking so that we will no longer have to resort to violence and war? What will it take to truly change our violent behavior and characteristics to that of peace, respect, and trust?

The world needs a radical revolution of values. This is not a new concept. The late great Rev. Martin Luther King, Jr. said this himself in a speech on April 4, 1967. We need to shift our values from material things ("thing-oriented society") to placing values and emphasis on people ("person-oriented society").[xxxiv]

In 2011, the United States Congress threatened to eliminate programs and services that government provided to the poor and needy during their debates over the national budget. Such things as programs for child care and medical care for the middle class, seniors and poor were proposed to be eliminated in favor of "privatizing" these programs and services. But they also favored retaining and adding more benefits and favors to the wealthy of the country. Yet, they wouldn't even reduce, in the slightest amount, their over indulgence in military spending which remains the largest portion of the national budget. For instance, in their time of "financial crisis" where the government could not even balance its own budget, the Federal Reserve loaned $25-billion to the Central Bank of Libya at an ultra-low interest rate of 0.025%.[xxxv] It charges the United States Treasury a much higher rate. Then, the United States citizens were required to pay, on the average, at least a 24-29% interest rate on their credit cards -- a nation that cannot even treat its own citizens right – not even with respect.

Governments should continually maintain the respect and trust of its citizens. When it loses this trust in favor of special interest, wealthy corporate executives and the rich, then it is time for wholesale changes – especially when the government has itself subverted ideals and principles of democracy. The people have every right, and should take upon themselves, to take destiny into their own hands and not be ruled by a tyrannical puppet government pulled by the strings of special interests. This behavior should not be tolerated in any society -- especially if these special interests have their own narrow agenda and uses government to fulfill their objectives.

Governments also have the bad habit of keeping things hidden from their citizens such as classifying documents as "top secret." Government should be free and open and accessible in every society. *Government is a servant to the people – not vice versa.* When government has reached a point where the people become servants to the regime, then it is time for change. The leadership no longer serves the people. For example, look at federal government hearings. On how many occasions are the public allowed to speak at these hearings? In municipal governments, the public are invited to speak during times allocated for "public comment." But actually, are these occasions available in state and federal legislative meetings? At your convenience, look at how hearings are conducted. Is the public invited to express their concerns on a given issue? Or, are selected individuals representing corporations or special interests invited to the hearings instead? Are these meetings really open? Is this really a true democracy? Do people really have a voice in their government? In this world of technology, has government maximized the latest technology to give its people a bigger participative voice in government?

Another bad behavior of man is his ability to manufacture weapons that kill. Yes, I'm talking about guns – rifles and pistols. Certainly rifles can serve a useful purpose for hunting, particularly for food. But assault weapons are really unfair to the game being hunted. The bad part of this scenario is that man has used these things against himself, to destroy his own species. He has used weapons of war designed to kill many people quickly -- sometimes in an organized fashion as in war, other times in unorganized manner as in random killings.

First of all, there would be no need for keeping a massive armament in the house if people did not live in paranoia – in fear for their lives. Unfortunately, in some countries, laws have been created to encourage the ownership of weapons. Such barbaric governance! Man must raise his level of thinking and accept the fact that all life is precious and valuable. Man has failed to remember that there is divinity in each human being. If each of us respect this thought, there would be no need for killing when we realize that all mankind is sacred.

Entities in the world have an agenda to reduce 90% of the world's population by poisoning the food chain and introducing harmful substances such as toxic medicine to mankind.[xxxvi] Humanity must protect itself from this mass genocide by waking up and being aware of everything around them. Being concerned for what is included in the water systems, what animals are fed before they are sent to slaughter, the pesticides that are used on vegetables, etc.

Furthermore, we must be wary of governments that undertake covert actions such as false flag operations in order to carry out hidden agendas. Some of the most powerful countries are guilty of doing these despicable acts against humanity. As citizens, we must demand accountability as to where all tax money is spent. Demand independent audits of everything that is spent in your country and know where your tax dollars are going. Continuously educate yourselves on political affairs lest you be run over by people who have agendas of their own – particularly if that agenda calls for your elimination.

The world can no longer tolerate secret societies in order for mankind to move forward. These secret organizations serve as stumbling blocks for the progression of mankind. Where it would be in the best interest for mankind to go in one direction, these secret societies will attempt to steer mankind in the opposite direction through deception, propaganda, and the use of military power (that they control). Do not fear, however, for the truth shall set mankind free.

Not only does the world need to adapt new values, but it needs to reassess its priorities. Do we want to continue to live in a world full of fear, hate, and violence? Or, do we want to create a world of peace, love, and tranquility?

CHAPTER 26
NEED FOR OPENNESS AND UNDERSTANDING

SHEDDING OUR EGOS

To move in the right direction, we must shed our personal and national pride by continuing to think that "we" are better than "they." Mankind's survival depends on all of us accepting each other as one. The first steps in doing this is that each of us needs to be open and understanding of one another. Yes, we have differences of cultures, ways of living, and a myriad of other things that would stand in our way of coming to a consensus.

We can overcome these differences by understanding that we are all human beings, foremost. The goal of mankind is its ultimate survival and sustainability. Each of us will bring certain gifts and talents to the table. Through these will come unique ideas that will benefit mankind in the long-term. All ideas and suggestions for moving mankind in the right direction should be weighed and considered carefully. But more importantly, they should be sought from every walk of life, from every corner of the world, regardless of social economic status or political or community position. Every individual should be encouraged to participate. After all, the objective is to uplift *all* of mankind.

Let's face it, we can debate the origins of the world forever. At this juncture, who's right or wrong is not important. The important matter at hand is the survival of mankind and leading us towards a sustainable world. This cannot be accomplished by trivial debate and argument especially with religious and political differences. The religions of the world must come together through tolerance and common understanding. We cannot move forward by keeping our heads buried in scripture. But the holy texts of the world will lead mankind towards freedom for the world if it is allowed to come alive by the mutual sharing of the sacred scriptures.

By the sharing of these ideals, we must all be open to the fact that some things are applicable in today's world and for the future, other things were more applicable to past times and should be abandoned. But through these scriptures, man can find common ground as a basis to begin new work and work commonly in a dynamic new direction.

Not only should we be open to other religious, political, and societal views, but we must also be open for scientific and technological contributions as well. Remember that God has given each of us special gifts. Some of these gifts include knowledge in science, technology and medicine and can be used dynamically for humanitarian purposes – not for a sinister plot to destroy mankind.

Open dialogue provides strength to the discussion whereas debate and argument weakens and slows progress. The important matter is to remain focused on the mission at hand. Whatever steps are taken to move mankind should be a peaceful transition without having to resort to violence.

But in the process of doing so, we must be vigilant at all times. Opposing entities will continue to attempt to disrupt the movement by placing its spies, intruders, and undercover agents in the process. They will do anything to derail the movement including shutting down lines of communications such as the Internet and perhaps even using military and police forces at their disposal. They may even attempt to use acts of intimidation to sway their agenda on the world. The people of the world must remain brave, courageous, and supportive of one another. Do not be fearful or intimidated. It will be like playing the game of chess – always plan your moves far in advance of your opponent. As God led the Jews out of the land of Egypt during the time of Pharaoh, He will lead and protect the masses of the world to freedom from oppression regardless of one's religion. But we must all be on the same page – united.

CHAPTER 27
OBEYING SPIRITUALITY'S GREATEST COMMANDMENT –

LOVE

"When the power of love overcomes the love of power, the world will know peace."
Jimi Hendrix

This is not a new hypothesis, it is a universal spiritual law which Jesus has commanded mankind – to love one another. Great spiritual leaders in modern times have reminded man of this law. Yet it has always been ignored and has fallen on deaf ears. It is a difficult law to follow if one continues isolate him/herself from the rest of the world; carry prejudicial thoughts; easily influenced by false information and perceptions about other people and cultures; misunderstand other religions; filled with negativity and full of hate.

God, in the person of Jesus, expressed unconditional love for the world and gave us the ability and power to love one another. However, throughout history, this has often been ignored. Nations continued to fight among each other. Powerful entities created their own agendas determining the fate of certain races and nationalities – some leading to the extermination of millions of people. Greed, power and money have a mysterious way of overshadowing our ability to love mankind.

We've become focused on material things rather than the good of people. Take for example the time when Jesus encountered the money changers in the temple. The money changers were not there to worship; they were there for selfish reasons – to make a profit. In modern times, the Republican majority in the United States Congress is doing everything it can to eliminate programs and services dedicated to the good of the people and the poor, but creating more favors for the wealthy. Yet, it seeks to maintain a sinful budget that supports a bloated war machine.

The only way to manifest peace in the world is to invest in love – not war. When countries continue to invest in war efforts and weapons, they continue to manifest and attract violence – not peace. These countries need to reprioritize their values, even if it takes the will of the people to cause this to happen. When love manifests itself in daily life, then there is no cause for living in paranoia and fear. But, when you continue to export violence, then the entire country lives in a world of fear – not love and peace; hence, the issues of terrorism.

As I have said before, to combat terrorism, don't give a reason for it to exist in the first place. If a nation continues to build arms and weapons, then it will attract terrorists. When a royal family is involved in drug trafficking, then it is time to rid the world of a monarchy doing unacceptable activities. Of course, in the new world, no one family should ever be placed on a pedestal since all of mankind will be equal.

Love gives us the power to be connected with each other, which in turn leads towards a greater understanding and appreciation of one another. It does not serve mankind well when a preacher in one country burns holy writ of another religion in defiance, disrespect, and misunderstanding of that religion – which then, sparks the unwarranted killing of innocent people in other parts of the country. Obviously, the command to love one another had been broken in this event. Justice should be served and such actions should not be tolerated. This was not a demonstration of freedom of speech and expression. It was a demonstration of hatred, bigotry and intolerance. Such actions serve as dead weight and only slow the progression of mankind's movement in the right direction.

When the power of love of over 95% of the world's population overcomes the love of power of only 5% of those who seek ultimate world control, only then will there be world peace. There will be a battle, but the righteous will prevail.

CHAPTER 28
MOVING TOWARD ONENESS

ONE WORLD – ONE NATION, ONE RACE

For too long, people of the world have remained separated by imaginary borders, man-made fences, and barriers designed to separate people and their countries. In history, governments made it extremely difficult to travel even within their own country. In order for mankind to survive, we must come together as one world – one nation, one race – the human race.

I am not advocating a singular world government run by tyrants whose agenda is to eliminate the 90% of the world's population. I advocate a democratic governmental architecture that serves all the people of the world and whose purpose is to edify mankind – not destroy it. The world has many unique traditions and cultures that should be saved, not destroyed. But yet, the world can come together as one world, the new "United Nations." Unlike the organization in New York, the new United Nations would ensure that wars would never be acceptable under any circumstance and that it would act as an intermediary to resolve disputes between nations. Of course, when the power of love prevails, there will be no disputes between nations for they would generally cooperate like the states of the United States.

There would be regional governments to act in a supervisory capacity of each "state." But generally representatives would be elected in free elections. And since there will be no currency to speak of, there will not be the inherent problems of political bribery or corruption. If so, these will not be tolerated.

Technology and social networking has brought the world closer together. There will be entities that will try to once again separate people by disrupting lines of communications. The people of the world cannot afford to allow this to happen. If necessary, backup systems should be activated should such an action occur.

The closer people of the world come together as one, the more powerful it they become. *The world is moving towards oneness*. It will take courage and determination by civic and religious leaders, lawyers, educators, artists, physicians, scientists, and working people of the world to move mankind in the right direction -- people who genuinely care for the well-being and future of humanity; people who share in one grand common vision regardless of one's religious or non-religious beliefs – but a genuine care for the survival and sovereignty of mankind. To build and fulfill that better world that we seek will require many summit meetings and conferences throughout the world. Some of it can be done virtually over the Internet. But the most important objective is to get every group that has a vision for a new and better world on the same page – to actually start to dialogue and discuss fulfilling these dreams and aspirations. Procrastinating will only be harmful because entities with their own agenda are already planning on executing their strategies to change the world to fit their own design – not necessarily in the best interest of mankind.

The quicker that people can move towards oneness, the better. And, there is an imperative element of timing at stake. This means that people of the world must be educated on the things that are happening in the world around them and what is about to come if they don't take a vested interest in their future as proverbial "doomsday" clock counts down.

As I said in my first book, the ultimate destruction of mankind will be brought off by man, not by God. If these entities are allowed to carry out their agenda, this will most likely happen sooner than later. It is important that mankind come together as one and begin to move in the right direction towards his grandest vision.

Jesus said: *"The Kingdom of Heaven is at hand."* (Mark 10:5-7). This is true. In some interpretations, it can be said that *"The Kingdom of God is at hand."* Either way, the people of the world have the power to bring the Kingdom of Heaven to Earth. This power has resided in mankind since the beginning of time. However, throughout time, he has forgotten about this particularly when he has often considered himself separate from God.

You don't have to be a priest or a pastor to be holy in your respective religion for this divinity has always resided within you. Man has never been separated from God. With God's powerful love, mankind can accomplish and overcome any obstacle including tyranny. But if he takes a careless, nonchalant attitude towards events, then tyranny will run him over. Realize and understand the power of love.

Therefore I admonish you to watch what you eat and drink. Be forever vigilant and question and scrutinize everything that your governments say and do.

Man originated over 50-60,000 years ago from its very

first "Adam(s)" in East Africa. Since that time, our ancestors have migrated out of that region to populate the world in the Middle East, Europe, Asia, Australia, North and South Americas. Other subsequent migrations have occurred since then. Genetically, we can all be linked together to the same common ancestry – the same tribe. We are all connected despite the illusional boundaries and borders that man has created through time which we have now come to know as nations. These barriers serve us, the human race, no purpose -- especially if we are members of "one family." Earth is "our home." Let us care for her wisely and respectfully.

God's will to establish the Kingdom of Heaven on Earth can be done. In preparing for the Lord's next coming, let it be so. Let us unite the world as never before. Let us come together as one world, one nation, one human race.

CHAPTER 29
YOU ARE HERE

THE PHYSICAL WORLD

Emanuel Swedenborg (1688-1772), scientist, philosopher, and Christian mystic best describes the universe in his book, *True Christianity – Volume 1,* a global concept of two worlds. One being a spiritual world where there are "angels and spirits" and a physical world where there are "people."

He describes both worlds having suns. The sun in the spiritual world is "pure love from Jehovah God, who is within that sun. The spiritual sun radiates heat and light. The essence of the heat it radiates is love, and the essence of the light is wisdom. That heat and light have an effect on people's wills and intellects. The heat affects the will; the light affects the intellect.

> *"The sun of the physical world is pure fire.*
> *As a result, the heat and the light from it*
> *are dead. Physical heat and light serve as a*
> *clothing for spiritual heat and light and as a*

device through which spiritual heat and light reach people.

In the spiritual world both the heat and the light radiate from the sun are substantial and are called spiritual. So are all the things in that world that come from that heat and light.

In the physical world, these two comparable things, the heat and the light, that radiate from this sun are material and are called physical. So are the things in this world that come about from this heat and light.

In both worlds there are three levels. They are called vertical levels. These result in the three areas where the three angelic heavens are set up. They also result in the three levels of the human mind, which correspond to the three angelic heavens. Everything else both here and there also has three levels.

There is a correspondence between things in the spiritual world and things in the physical world.

There is a design that has been built into each and every thing in each world.

First we need to get an overall idea about the above. Otherwise the human mind in its utter ignorance of all this, easily slips into the idea that the universe was created by nature, and only out of respect for the authority of the church will it say that nature was created by God. If people do not know how God created nature, when they take a deep look at the subject they slip headfirst into a materialist philosophy that denies God." [xxxvii]

Emanuel Swedenborg

We must understand precisely where we are currently at in this universe. If you are reading this book, *you are in the physical world*. The physical world can be very much like that of the spiritual world or which many of us refer to as "Heaven." But there are many obstacles and barriers that prevent us from creating this reality. First of all, many of us have separated ourselves from God; and have adopted a materialist philosophy; allowing communications from evil spiritual worlds to influence our lives. Yes, Swedenborg talks about three levels. Some may interpret these three levels as Heaven, Earth, and Hell. Others may interpret these three levels as the "trinity" within oneself. As I had said earlier, it takes three points to live a balanced life. Many are living only on two axis – spinning out of balance.

We all have the power to create heaven on Earth, but we must come to the realization that we all have to undergo a significant "makeover" in our individual and collective lives. I am not saying that everyone has to become Christian for each individual on this planet has a significant role in building this physical world. But we must not let negative influences divide mankind and serve as barriers in building the paradise that it can become.

I am not going to argue whether or not the Last Judgment has taken place as Emanuel Swedenborg suggested in 1757 though only in the spiritual world had he witnessed it[xxxviii] and followed by the Second Coming of Jesus Christ, not in person, but by a revelation of Him through the inner spiritual sense of the Word[xxxix] through Swedenborg.[xl] I wasn't alive then to serve witness to it or not. And, I don't want to shatter the dreams and aspirations of millions who are still expecting His "Second Coming" even if the event may have already taken place. Nevertheless, time has moved forward and there are pressing issues that still remain for mankind -- much of which is still slowing the progression of humanity regardless of what may have already happened in the historic spiritual realms.

The greatest challenge among us in the physical world is to unite as one human race – not by a singular, one-world government -- but through a common understanding of our roles. A common global government by the people and for the people would be ideal. Not a form based on tyranny, dictated by profit and greed, but a form of government built on the principles of democracy. But in order to do this, we must all understand that we are all connected as I have said in previous chapters.

Swedenborg explains this beautifully in his book...

> *"Now to say how the Word allows people throughout all parts of the world to experience the presence of, and a connection to, the Lord, and heaven. To the Lord the entire angelic heaven is like one person. The same is true for the church across the earth. The church where the Word is read and where the Lord is therefore known is like the heart and the lungs in that human being. The Lord's heavenly kingdom is like the heart, and his spiritual*

kingdom is like the lungs. Just as all the other limbs, internal organs, and parts of the human body have life and continued existence because of these two fountains of life, so, too, all the people around the world who have a religion, worship one God, and live good lives have life and continued existence because the church is connected to the Lord and heaven through the Word. Non-Christians are in that human being and play the part of its limbs and internal organs outside the thorax that holds the heart and lungs. Non-Christians have life from the Lord through heaven because the Word in the Christian church, just as the limbs and organs throughout the body have life because of the heart and lungs. There is also a similar exchange between them.

This is also the reason why Christians who read the Word make up the chest of that (giant) human being. They are in fact central among all people. Surrounding them are Catholics. Surrounding the Catholics are Muslims who acknowledge the Lord as the greatest prophet or the Son of God. Farther out than these are Africans. People and nations in the Middle East and the Indies make up the farthest circumference.

One can determine that the whole of heaven is like this from a similar situation that exists in every individual community in heaven. Every community is a heaven in a smaller form, but a form that is nonetheless human. In every community in heaven, angels who are at the center of the community similarly play the role of the heart and the lungs. They have the most light. That light and a resulting awareness of truth spread out and give them spiritual life. It was once demonstrated that when the angels at the center, who constitute the realm of the heart and lungs and who have the most light, were taken way, the angels around them came into an intellectual shadow and into so little awareness of truth that they started lamenting. As soon as the central angel returned, however, the others saw light again and had the awareness of truth they had before."[xli]

I am going to deviate from Swedenborg's observation about Africans. Since the time he wrote his book, much has been learned about genetics and deep ancestry. Africans should be considered as central and not "farther out" as Swedenborg has expressed. In fact, Africans are closer to us than you think. They may be very well the "core" of our existence. As I have mentioned in the previous chapter, all of our deep ancestries have originated in Africa. All of us have a deep link via our DNA to an African heritage regardless whether we believe we originally came from Europe, Asia, the Middle East, the Americas, or elsewhere. The original "Garden of Eden" may very well be centered in a region in East Africa. If you don't believe this, I invite you to have your deep ancestry researched.

Regardless of our deep ancestry, each of us has the Light within us regardless of whether we are Christians or

Non-Christians; believers or non-believers; regardless of sexual orientation or gender – heterosexual or homosexual. *Every human being has the Light of God within them.* This is what makes us uniquely connected to each other. This is what makes each individual uniquely divine. When we use religion or any other reason to war against each other, we literally destroy parts of our own body – our own hearts, lungs, limbs, and internal organs (i.e. civil wars). Why do you desire to destroy your divine physical body – to put it through such torment, torture, and suffering? Buddhists have taught us that life is full of suffering. Suffering does not have to be a condition of life if mankind wills it so. But it must understand what causes suffering and overcome the forces that cause these conditions to destroy our lives – our hearts and lungs. Suffering exist in the world as long as it is still tolerated by mankind. Humanity no longer has to tolerate suffering by removing barriers and obstacles that create suffering and move forth to build a physical world like that in heaven.

The first and foremost obstacle is not to be deceived by negativity and forces that will attempt to convince you that such a goal is not attainable. These people are in government, education, as well as churches. As Swedenborg explains:

> *"Be very careful, then, not to convince yourself that you are alive from yourself – do not think you are wise, have faith, are loving, perceive truth, or will or do with what is good from yourself. As people do convince themselves of these things, they cast their mind down from heaven to earth and change from being spiritual to being oriented to nature, their own senses, and their own body. They close*

the higher regions of their mind. Doing so
blinds them to everything having to do with
God, heaven, or the church. Then whatever
they happen to think, reason, or say on these
subjects is ridiculous, because they are in the
dark. At the same time, ironically, they gain
greater confidence in the wisdom of their
perspective. Since the higher regions of their
mind are closed, where then true light of life
makes its home, a lower region of their mind
opens up that is attuned only to the glimmer
of the world. That glimmer devoid of light
from the higher regions, is faint and deceptive.
In it, false things seem true and true things
false; argumentation on false premises seems
like wisdom, and on true premises seems like
madness. People like this truly believe they
have the visual powers of an eagle, when
in fact they cannot see what comes from
wisdom any more than a bat can see in broad
daylight."[xlii]

Emanuel Swedenborg

We in the physical world have a duty to build a better
life not only for ourselves, but to ensure that generations to
come will enjoy a better life than we experience today -- a life
of peace and tranquility, devoid of war, pestilence, poverty
and homelessness. There are people in this world that enjoy
seeing people suffer. They go out of their way to ensure
suffering in the world through deceitful practices, false and
misleading statements that appear as "truths." Even to the
extent of limiting the world's monetary resources through

hoarding and over taxation of the lesser classes in society all to benefit their luxurious life styles.

The will of the people can get rid of suffering in the world when they realize that they have been misled and have the power to correct the course of the world for the better through peaceful means. People in "authority" would normally rely on weapons and force to prevent changes through violence and then lead people to believe that the peaceful movement had been the cause of all violence. If the famous chef, Jamie Oliver, could successfully and peacefully change the political environment of the Los Angeles City School District and open their eyes and raise awareness for the need for better diet and nutrition in their schools though his "Food Revolution," then people of the world can peacefully change the world by chipping away at things that don't work and are wrong in society. The ultimate "authority" rests with the people -- not through government, corporations, political leaders, they the military, or police forces.

Changes in this physical world are constantly occurring -- some rapidly, others gradually. Some environmental changes will not benefit mankind and humanity must be cognizant of these developments which will eventually modify the face of the Earth. Because of pure greed, money and politics, man has failed to heed warnings of global warming. Due to his failure to control pollution, polar ice caps are melting, causing oceans to rise. It is said that within this century, sea levels will rise as much as 50 feet or more.

This means that cities along the coastlines in all countries will be submerged underwater. Cities like Miami, New York, Tokyo, and London. All cities at sea level will be underwater.

I am not in a position to build an arc like Noah to accommodate multi-millions of people around the world. But if I am able to spread this word way in advance, then moving mankind in the right direction to safety will have succeeded. I encourage you to move to higher ground -- the highest point on your continent. To many, this will be a long journey. So, travel light and carry only what you need. This need not be a mass exodus out of pure panic and hysteria – but should be carried out calmly and peacefully. But be careful of what the Bible once referred to as "highwaymen."[xliii] In modern times, these people can be considered as "con artists" and "thieves." Protect yourselves during your journey. God will be with you always.

CHAPTER 30
CLOSING THOUGHTS

After I completed *Kami Jin,* I shelved the prequel to that book due to the urgency of getting this book to market after witnessing current events and things that I have seen on the Internet, radio, television and newspapers.

Knowing how the masses will behave in times of an emergency, people are generally reluctant to act on an idea or suggestion if they perceive that there is no danger until the danger absolutely presents itself. By then, it's way too late. Forces will have already worked behind the scenes creating the stage for greater things to happen by making subtle changes before peoples' eyes. Like a skillful magician, changes will occur without the people's knowledge until the surprise is sprung upon the masses. The people are then stunned, horrified with disbelief. But by then, it can be a matter of life or death.

It is my hope with this book to bring people and factions together. Many groups of people have very good visions for the world. But there are common problems inherent in all. Barriers such as personal and corporate beliefs inhibit openness and the willingness to accept other opinions and views freely. Some automatically reject ideas because of certain other beliefs without evaluating the whole concept or idea. We need to come together in open dialogue and start building and planning our future. But we need to start taking steps in building our future lest a certain minority made up of a few very powerful and influential people in governments and corporations shatter our dreams and aspirations and proceed with their vision of a not-so-bright world that may be totally opposite of what we envision, nor what God has envisioned for humanity.

Perhaps I will not be able to move all of mankind in the right direction. As with horses in a burning barn, there will be some stubborn creatures that will refuse to move. Hopefully, I will be able to move humanity towards safety that mankind in the entire world will be able to enjoy God's vision.

Man has the ability to ensure that God's Vision becomes a reality. He has given us the power to implement that vision here in the physical world if we collectively take the power and carry it out. How? As I've hinted throughout this book – by coming together on common grounds and mutual dialogue and exchange of ideas -- to make man's grandest vision for life in this physical world a reality. Not by one country or a small group of people – but collectively, by the people of the world acting as one – one race – the human race regardless of nationality, color and religion. The Kingdom of Heaven *is* at hand -- *it rests in the hands of humanity.*

In closing, as the world comes together, let us adopt a universal "Bill of Rights." Rights that humans around the world can cherish and enjoy equally no matter and wherever they may be in the world. As Satori Dennis Agape so eloquently listed on his post in Facebook on February 8, 2011:

THE RIGHTS

We All have Rights.

The Right To Life.
The Right To Privacy.
The Right To Responsibility.
The Right To Choices.

The Right To Childhood.
The Right To Play, The Pursuit of Happiness, Joy and
Celebration.
The Right To Education, Knowledge, Wisdom, Self-
Development, Awareness.
The Right To ones own unique identity.

The Right To Nationality, Race and Culture.
The Right To Form Family Bonds and Relationships.
The Right To Community and Involvement.
The Right To Protect Oneself, Family, Possessions from
harm.
The Right To Love and Care for Whom we choose.
The Right To Love And Be Loved.
The Right To Respect, Honor, Courtesy, Dignity.
The Right To Better oneself at no expense on others or other's
rights.
The Right To Choices of One's Life in direct accordance to
the Rights.

The Right To Ownership of Property.
The Right To Seek A Safe Place To Live.
The Right To Share Resources.

The Right To Take Care of the Environment and those who share it.

The Right To Freedom of Movement and Residence.
The Right To Freedom of Thought, Feelings and Beliefs.
The Right To Art, Creativity, Self-Expression.
The Right To Worship and Practice of One's Beliefs in direct accordance to the Rights.
The Right To Pursue one's purpose in direct accordance to the Human Rights.
The Right To Truth.
The Right To Know.
The Right To Pursue our Paths Of the Heart.
The Right To Change Our Beliefs in accordance to who we are and the Rights.

The Right To Social Security.
The Right To Be Cared for when one has difficulty taking care of oneself.
The Right To Food, Water, Shelter and Safety.
The Right To Contribute to The Welfare of oneself and others.
The Right To Good Health and Well Being.
The Right To Proper Health Care.
The Right To A Fair and Free World.
The Right To Gift unhindered by the government and by law.

The Right To Work and Protection from Unfair Labor practices.
The Right To Proper Acknowledgement of one's creation, contribution, work and accomplishment.

The Right To Fair Compensation For Work or Service Provided.

The Right To Public and Private Assembly.
The Right To Democracy and participation in government.
The Right To A Fair Trial and Arbitration.
The Right Of No Unfair Detainment.
The Right To Fair Treatment.
The Right To Justice, Mercy, Forgiveness and Atonement.
The Right To The Protection of the Rights By Law.
The Right To The Rights regardless of any discriminatory factor.
The Right To The Rights regardless of location.
The Right To Proper Justice when Rights are violated.
The Right Of No False Witness in violation of the Rights.
The Right To Seek Fair and Just recourse for Violation of Rights.

Therefore, it doesn't matter whether we were created according to the Biblical version of Genesis by the accounts of Adam and Eve; if we evolved from Adams and Eves by a tribe or tribes of people that lived in certain part of world that we now know as East Africa; or, even if we evolved from other life forms. More importantly, let us concentrate on the present and look forward towards the future. Let not our differences serve as barriers for the progress of humanity.

Let us shed our hatred against people of other cultures, religions, traditions, beliefs, color, and sexual orientation. Rather, let us begin to build relationships and bridges of embracing love through a global conversation of peace that will bring about universal change in the world -- a change that will benefit all of humanity. Let us mend God's tapestry, not tear it apart.

Let us rid the world of poverty and homelessness by eliminating root causes – for there are many. Many people hold onto these causes like a child with a security blanket. It is time to abandon the blanket and start walking as a mature, intellectual adult. We cannot hold onto the things that do not serve us well nor serve humanity with equality for all – not the proverbial fable of "equal opportunity."

Let us dissolve governments that no longer serve the people well and peacefully replace them with representation committed to serving the people – not special interests, political parties or ideals, free from corruption, financial influence and the voracity of control and dictatorial power – with governments driven by common sense, not by the whims of social classes, business leaders, or select scholars, but by the people and genuinely for the people. Governments that will lay down arms, make the concept of war obsolete, tear down borders, and genuinely build bridges and highways for peace among all nations.

Finally, let us spiritually bring together life, art, education, science, and culture into harmony recognizing that each of these are and will always be inspired by God. The problems that face the world can be solved spiritually – not politically, economically, or religiously, but through pure common sense as we return to the basics: "Do to others as you want them to do to you."

Thus, I present to you, A Vision for Humanity. Let us all move mankind in the right direction.

RECOMMENDED READING

Choosing Honor – An American Woman's Search for God, Family and Country in an Age of Corruption. Mary T. Ficalora. Avail Press, Calabasas, CA 91302

The Middle Theory – A Guide to Balance. Deshon M. Fox. Author House, Bloomington, IN, 2009.

True Christiantiy – Volume 1. Emanuel Swedenborg. Swedenborg Foundation, West Chester, PA, 2010.

True Christiantiy – Volume 2. Emanuel Swedenborg. Swedenborg Foundation Press, West Chester, PA, 2011.

Heaven and Hell. Emanuel Swedenborg. Swedenborg Foundation, West Chester, PA, 2010.

If the Church Were Christian – Rediscovering the Values of Jesus. Philip Gulley. Harper One, New York, NY 10022.

MORE ABOUT
THE AUTHOR

JASON SHOHARA, AUTHOR

Author and screenwriter, Jason Shohara, has published his science fiction novel *Kami Jin* in 2009 as an e-book through Smashwords, and as a paperback in 2010 through Wordclay. He is a former staff writer for *Drum Corps News,* and has written for various other magazines, newsletters and blogs. He also is a member of the Greater Los Angeles Writers Society and has a Bachelor of Arts degree in Creative Writing from California State University, Long Beach and has studied creative writing under Dora Beale Polk. He has studied screenwriting through the Open Door Program sponsored by the Writers Guild of America, West in Los Angeles. Jason has judged screenplays for the Honolulu, Mexico, and Las Vegas international film festivals.

He has been active in civic government as a commissioner, board member on non-profit organizations, and is a political activist striving for social and economic justice and equality for the homeless. Although happily married with family, he also supports LGBT issues, having longtime friends and acquaintances in this community. Jason has worldwide friends, fans and supporters on Facebook, Twitter, LinkedIn, and MySpace. Jason is very highly spiritual, but is also fascinated with science, medicine and politics. As for his political and religious views, he considers himself totally independent – a Universalist.

Jason has studied behavioral science, psychology, and adult education through his educational experiences at the University of California at Los Angeles.

Jason was bestowed the 2010 People's Choice Award by Million Dollar Book Reviews.

For more information, visit his website at www. lloydkaneko.com.

Discover other titles by Jason Shohara (aka Lloyd Kaneko) at Smashwords.com:

*Kami Jin - **https://www.smashwords. com/books/view/4075***

Connect with Jason Online:

Twitter: http://www.twitter.com/jashohara

Facebook: http://www.facebook.com/AuthorLloydKaneko

Smashwords: https://www.smashwords. com/profile/view/kamijin1951

MySpace: http://www.myspace.com/lkaneko

LinkedIn: http://www.linkedin.com/profile/ view?id=46172635&trk=tab_pro

Google+: https://plus.google. com/109508284445487951408/posts?hl=en

Pinterest: http://www.pinterest.com/jassho

My Blogs: http://creativeartistskettle.blogspot.com

http://www.kamijin1951.blogspot.com

Website: http://www.lloydkaneko.com

ENDNOTES

[i] *Black Ops Whistleblower Exposes Alien Takeover Agenda - See more at:* http://www.collective-evolution.com/2013/07/12/black-ops-whistleblower-exposes-alien-takeover-agenda/#

[ii] Let Us Reason Ministries, *History and Timeline of Its Founders* (2009), Retrieved August 3, 2010, http://www.letusreason.org/Cult11.htm.

[iii] "Radioactive Tuna Caught Off California Coast." *Liberals Unite,* August 24, 2013. http://samuel-warde.com/2013/08/radioactive-bluefin-tuna-caught-off-california-coast/

[iv] Cenzon, Rod. *Circle,* "What is the Role of Reiyukai in Your Life,"- Summer, 1977.

[v] *Population "Control" New World Order Style. Ken Adachi Educate-Yourself – The Freedom of Knowledge, The Power of Thought.* http://educate-yourself.org/nwo/nwopopcontrol.shtml

[vi] Patrick Henry, March 1799.

[vii] Tom McBride and Ron Nief, "The Beloit College Mindset List for the Class of 2014," 2010, http://www.beloit.edu/mindset/index.php

[viii] Citizens United v. Federal Election Commission, No. 08-205 (U. S. Jan. 21, 2010).

[ix] "Microchip Mind Control Implants and Cybernetics." Rauni-Leena Luukanen-Kilde, M.D. December 6, 2000. *Rense.com*. http://rense.com/general17/imp.htm

[x] "Microwave Mind Control" by Tim Rifat (http://www.whale.to/b/rifat.html)

[xi] "U.S.A. Puppet of Private Bankers – Alex Jones" http://youtu.be/JZtcn6HC0FA.

[xii] *Synopsis of the Alien Master Plan*. http://www.montalk.net/alien/35/synopsis-of-the-alien-master-plan

[xiii] *The Middle Theory – A Guide to Balance*. Deshon M. Fox. AuthorHouse, Bloomington, Indiana (2009)

[xiv] "We Are All Connected," Symphony of Science. YouTube.com, http://www.youtube.com/watch?v=XGK84Poeynk&feature=related

[xv] "U.S. and Iran Agree to Speed Talks to Defuse Nuclear Issue." *New York Times – Middle East*. http://www.nytimes.com/2013/09/28/world/obama-says-he-spoke-to-irans-president-by-phone.html?_r=0

[xvi] "The Venus Project – Beyond Politics, Poverty and War: "Resource Based Economy," 2009, Jaque Fresco, http://www.thevenusproject.com/a-new-social-design/resource-based-economy

[xvii] The Eightfold Path of Buddhism. *For Dummies*. Rabbi Marc Gellman and Monsignor Thomas Hartman. Religion for Dummies Cheat Sheet. http://www.dummies.com/how-to/content/the-eightfold-path-of-buddhism.html

[xviii] The Genographic Project. National Geographic. https://genographic.nationalgeographic.com/about/

[xix] Genesis 1:26

[xx] "Wisconsin Assembly Passes Anti-Union Bill as State Democrats Stay Away." New York Times. February 26, 2011. http://www.nytimes.com/2011/02/26/us/26wisconsin.html?_r=0

[xxi] The Venus Project – Beyond Politics, Poverty and War. http://www.thevenusproject.com.

[xxii] "20 Medical Studies That Prove Cannabis Can Cure Cancer." *Collective Evolution*. August 23, 2013. Arjun Walia. http://www.collective-evolution.com/2013/08/23/20-medical-studies-that-prove-cannabis-can-cure-cancer/

[xxiii] "Why I Changed My Mind on Weed." Dr. Sanjay Gupta, Chief Medical Correspondent. *CNN Health*. August 8, 2013. http://www.cnn.com/2013/08/08/health/gupta-changed-mind-marijuana/

[xxiv] "So What Really Is In a McDonald's Chicken McNugget?" Author Unknown. Rense.com. 5-14-7. http://rense.com/general76/chk.htm

[xxv] "School Lunch and Breakfast Programs." Nutrion.gov. http://www.nutrition.gov/food-assistance-programs/school-lunch-and-breakfast-programs

[xxvi] "Costa Mesa Employee Commits Suicide at City Hall" *Voice of OC*. Laguna Lou. April 6, 2011. http://www.voiceofoc.org/countywide/county_government/article_bb2d33ba-5119-11e0-b488-001cc4c03286.html?mode=jqm_com

[xxvii] "Lex Scantinia." *Wikipedia*. http://en.wikipedia.org/wiki/Lex_Scantinia

[xxviii] *Homosexuality. The Bible, The Truth: The Bible Does Not Condemn Homosexuality. Wayne Gray. Xlibris.* http://books.google.com/books?id=w2GQO8CbBMgC&pg=PT172&lpg=PT172&dq=Council+of+Elvira+homosexuality&source=bl&ots=P32U5HEEZA&sig=Q

a9HATxNcuQ69H8SsEsCGYSFXeU&hl=en&sa=X
&ei=Y9ZtUp2JIqb7yAHVpYG4Dw&ved=0CEgQ6A
EwBg#v=onepage&q=Council%20of%20Elvira%20
homosexuality&f=false

[xxix] *Christianity – Social Tolerance and Homosexuality.
John Boswell. University of Chicago Press.* http://books.
google.com/books?id=v-MR5_AdG68C&pg=PA178&d
q=Council+of+Ancyra+homosexuality&hl=en&sa=X&
ei=iNltUoj2COGbygGu_oGYAQ&ved=0CDkQ6AE
wAg#v=onepage&q=Council%20of%20Ancyra%20
homosexuality&f=false

[xxx] *Is it a Choice? Answers to the Most Frequently Asked
Questions About Gay and Lesbian People. Eric Marcus.
San Francisco. Harper. 2005.*

[xxxi] "Sexual Selection," Genetics Glossary, National
Geographic, The Genographic Project, https://
genographic.nationalgeographic.com/genographic/lan/
en/glossary.html (1996)

[xxxii] "How Many Americans Have A Passport?"
The Expeditioner. January 22, 2013. http://www.
theexpeditioner.com/2010/02/17/how-many-americans-
have-a-passport-2/#

[xxxiii] "Introducing The Free World Charter." The Zeitgeist
Movement Official Blog. December 2, 2011. http://
blog.thezeitgeistmovement.com/blog/colin-turner/
introducing-free-world-charter

[xxxiv] "Beyond Vietnam – A Time to Break Silence." Martin
Luther King, Jr. April 6, 1967. American Rhetoric
Online Speech Bank. http://www.americanrhetoric.
com/speeches/mlkatimetobreaksilence.htm

[xxxv] "Libya-Owned Banking Corp. Drew At Least $5
Billion from Fed in Crisis." Donal Griffin & Bob Ivry.
Bloomberg. April 1, 2011. http://www.bloomberg.com/

news/2011-03-31/libya-owned-arab-banking-corp-drew-at-least-5-billion-from-fed-in-crisis.html

[xxxvi] "The Population Reduction Agenda for Dummies." Paul Joseph Watson. June 26, 2009. Alex Jones' Prison Planet.com. http://www.prisonplanet.com/the-population-reduction-agenda-for-dummies.html

[xxxvii] "The Creation of the Universe," *True Christianity, pg. 100-101,* Emanuel Swedenborg, Swedenborg Foundation, Inc. (West Chester, Pennsylvania, 2010).

[xxxviii] *Emanuel Swedenborg, The Last Judgment and Babylon Destroyed. All the Predictions in the Apocalypse are This Day Fulfilled. (Swedenborg Foundation, 1952, Paragraphs 1-74)*

[xxxix] *Emanuel Swedenborg, The True Christian Religion: Containing the Universal Theology of The New Church Foretold by the Lord in Daniel 7:13 and in Revelation 21:1,2 (Swedenborg Foundation 1952, paragraphs 193-215)*

[xl] *True Christian Religion, paragraphs 753-786*

[xli] Emanuel Swedenborg,"Because of the Word, Even People Who Are outside the Church and Who Do Not Have the Word Have Light," *True Christianity*, Swedenborg Foundation, (West Chester, Pennsylvania, 2010 pg. 334-335)

[xlii] Emanuel Swedenborg, "The Essence of God: Divine Love and Wisdom," *True Christianity,* Swedenborg Foundation, Inc. (West Chester, Pennsylvania, 2011), pg. 59.

[xliii] Luke 10:30